PREPOSTEROUS

A Richard Jackson Book

ALSO BY PAUL B. JANECZKO

PREPOSTEROUS
POEMS OF YOUTH

Selected by Paul B. Janeczko

11/12/93

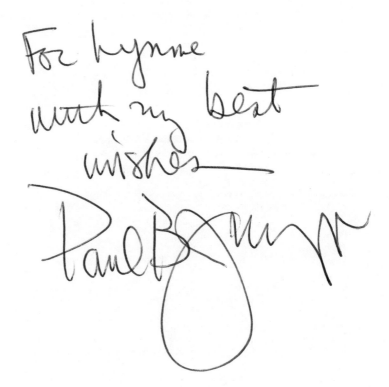

For Lynne
with my best
wishes—
Paul B. Janeczko

ORCHARD BOOKS   NEW YORK

Orchard Books
95 Madison Avenue
New York, NY 10016

Manufactured in the United States of America
Book design by Mina Greenstein
The text of this book is set in 11 pt. Fournier.
10 9 8 7 6 5 4 3 2

Library of Congress Cataloging-in-Publication Data
Janeczko, Paul B.
Preposterous / selected by Paul B. Janeczko.
p.   cm.   Includes index.
Summary: An anthology of poetry about being a teenager
and adolescent problems and concerns.
ISBN 0-531-05901-4   ISBN 0-531-08501-5 (lib. bdg.)
1. Young adult poetry, American. 2. Teenagers—
Poetry. [1. Adolescence—Poetry. 2. American poetry—
Collections.] I. Title. PS586.3.J37 1991
811.008'09283—dc20 90-39644 CIP AC

For my friends,
Tom McBride & Bob Skapura,
who have carried adolescence
into middle age
with zest, style, and good cheer,
although at times with questionable taste.

CONTENTS

Zip on "Good Advice"

■ *Gary Hyland*

What do parents know anyhow?
Been here twice as long as us
and what do they have to say?
Do your homework, Marvin.
Nothing ventured, nothing gained.

They got these golden oldies
lines to lead your life by—
A penny saved is a penny earned.
A stitch in time saves nine.

So is that the big IT?
The wisdom of the ages
funneled into one brain
centuries of progress
in grungy slippers chirpin'
at seven in the mornin'
Rise and shine, Marvin.
The early bird gets the worm!

Dodo

■ *Henry Carlile*

Years they mistook me for you,
chanting your name in the streets,
pointing grubby fingers.
Today in the natural history museum
I saw why.
Dodo, you look the way I feel,
with your sad absentminded eyes
and your beak like a stone-age ax.
Even your feathers
dingy and fuzzy.
What woman would want them for a hat?

With a name like *Didus ineptus*
where could you go,
wings too small to fly with
and feet so large and slow?
You were not very palatable.
Men slaughtered you for sport.
Hogs ate the one egg you laid each year.
Sometimes I think I know how it feels
to be scattered over the world,
a foot in the British Museum,
a head in Copenhagen,
to be a lesson after the fact,
an entity in name only,
and that taken in vain.

high school

■ *George Roberts*

while the school's star athletes
snap down beer on country roads
and later stumble into basement parties
(where once   to prove a boast
donna mccarthy   for the briefest of moments
removed her blouse)

scrut does his homework
thinks about the justice of letter jackets
and pronounces another final judgment
on his friends

all the while wishing
he shared their easy way
with books and rules
with colt 45 malt liquor
and with the electric skin
of donna mccarthy

Orphanage Boy

■ *Robert Penn Warren*

From the orphanage Al came to
Work on the farm as what you'd call
Hired boy if he got enough to
Call hire. Back at the woodpile chop-
ping stove-lengths, he taught me all the
Dirty words I'd never heard of
Or learned from farm observation,
And generally explained how
Folks went in for fun, adding that
A farm was one hell of a place
For finding fun.

Polite enough,
He'd excuse himself after sup-
per and go sit on the stile with
Bob, the big white farm bulldog, close
At his side, and watch the sun sink
Back of the barn or maybe, in
The opposite direction, the
Moon rise.

It was a copperhead
Bit Bob, and nothing, it looked like,
Would make him better. Just after
Supper one night my uncle stood
On the front porch and handed a
Twelve-gauge to Al and said, "Be sure
You do it right back of the head."
He never named Bob's name.

Al's face
Was white as clabber, but he took
The gun, not saying a word, just
Walking away down the lane to-
ward sunset, Bob too, me follow-
ing. Then, in the woods where it was
Nigh dark, he did it. He gave me
The gun, smoke still in the muzzle,
Said, "Git away, you son-a-bitch,"
And I got away and he lay
On the dead leaves crying even
Before I was gone.

That night he
Never came home and the Sheriff
Never found him.

It was six months
Before I went back in the woods
To the place. There was a real grave
There. There was a wood cross on the
Grave. He must have come back to the
Barn for the shovel and hammer,
And back again to hang them up.

It must have taken nigh moonset.

Stay with Me

■ *Garrett Kaoru Hongo*

At six o'clock, most people
already sitting down to dinner
and the evening news, Gloria's
still on the bus, crying
in a back seat, her face
bathed in soft blue light
from the fluorescent lamps.
She leans her head down
close to her knees, tugs
at the cowl of her raincoat
so it covers her eyes, tries
to mask her face and stifle
the sobbing so the young black
in the seat across the aisle
won't notice her above the
disco music pouring from
his radio and filling the bus.
He does anyway, and, curious,
bends toward her, placing a hand
on her shoulder, gently,
as if consoling a child
after the first disappointment,
asking, "Is it cool, baby?"

She nods, and, reassured,
he starts back to his seat,
but she stops him, sliding
her hand over his, wanting
to stroke it, tapping it instead,
rhythmically, as if his hand
were a baby's back and she
its mother, singing and rocking
it softly to sleep. The black
wishes he could jerk his hand
away, say something hip to save
himself from all that's not
his business, something like
"Get back, Mama! You a fool!"
but he can't because Gloria's
just tucked her chin over
both their hands, still resting
on her shoulder, clasped them
on the ridge of her jaw the way
a violinist would hold a violin.

He can feel the loose skin
around her neck, the hard bone
of her jaw, the pulse
in her throat thudding against
his knuckles, and still he wants
to pull away, but hesitates,
stammers, asks again,
"Hey . . . Is it okay?"

He feels something hot
hit his arm, and, too late
to be startled now, sighs
and gives in, turning his
hand over, lifting it, clasping
hers, letting her bring it
to her cheek, white and slick
with tears, stroking her face
with the back of his hand,
rubbing the hollow of her cheek
against his fist, and she,

speaking finally, "Stay with me
a little while. Till your stop?
Just stay with me," as her face
blooms and his shines
in the blue fluorescent light.

Economics

■ *Robert Wrigley*

He learned economics in the shade
of a flatbed truck, owned by the man
he worked for, who owned as well the tons
of concrete on it, the farm never farmed
but mowed, the Ford dealership in town,
a great white house across the way, and a daughter
there with her friends, sunbathing by the pool.
A ton of cement in hundred-pound bags
he'd already stacked on pallets in the barn.
It was Saturday, after lunch; sun seared
his neck and shoulders, flickered
from the drops on the girls by the pool,
and shone in the suffocating dust
he saw through. Though his eyes were closed
when the kick hit his heels,
he wasn't sleeping. He was awake
and dreaming in the splashes and laughter,
resting in the dust and truck-smelling
shade, leaned against a gritty rear wheel.

And so it was the joy he imagined
tied then to the owner's sneer
and warning. Joy, and the rage he let build
through a ton and a half of lifting
and lugging, the loathing for a man
who owned all that he could see
from high on the back of a flatbed truck,
sweeping dust into the air
and watching when the man came out

to the pool, soft and flabby,
and grinned through an oafish cannonball
that made the girls laugh, applauding like seals.
It was a rage that cooked in his old
black car, that ground in its slow start,
and lunged like its badly slipping clutch.
He longed in his sweat for speed and oblivion,
the thrum of good tires, the deep-lunged roar
of power, a wheel in his hands
like a weapon, turn by premeditated turn.

"You best work, boy, or your whole life'll be
as shitty as today." When the kick had come
he flinched, involuntarily. His one knee rose,
his left arm blocked his face, and in the grit
of his right glove his fist closed on
the readiness to hit. He was ashamed
to be caught, ashamed for his flinch,
ashamed he could not, as the owner glared down
at his startled eyes, leap to his feet and murder him.
He was ashamed by his silence, by the ache
even then in his back and arms, the guilt
he could never disprove. The route home
that day derided him, maddeningly slow
through marginal farms and identical suburbs.
His mother's howdy-do repulsed him,
and his father's little wink seemed the grimace
of a ninny. It was Saturday night,
he had no date, but didn't sleep until morning,
when he rose anyway, hating his face in the mirror.

Monday, washing as always the endless line
of new cars, he began to understand
the limitations of revenge: murder, fire,
the daughter's humiliation at school—
these were risks he couldn't take. Even scratches
here and there on the cars. He cursed his luck
and scrubbed, twisted the chamois so tightly
it tore, and Sven, the old one-armed Swede
he worked with, shook his head and sighed.
"You just wash, Hercules," he said. "I'll dry 'em."

So he went on, lathering and scrubbing,
quiet, old Sven telling dirty jokes,
analyzing the bouquet, the savor of women,
offering his wisdom in every field
until the boy threw down his sponge, spit,
looked the old man deeply in the eye,
and asked him in all his feeble goddamn brilliance
what the hell was he doing here, washing cars
a half a buck a crack with a boy.

And when he saw Sven's face change
it almost came out, all the simple story
about sweat and mistakes, cement and rage
and the long ride to nowhere through a life
he couldn't stand. What would it have taken
for the shame to come out, the shame
now for hurting a poor old man, for kicking—
in his own little way—as sure as any
cool and flabby man who owned a world.
Instead the boy worked, behind him
Sven mopping up, silent until the last three sedans,
when he flipped the chamois on a hood and said
"Here, goddamn ye. I'm tired. You finish 'em."
And so he was alone at the end,
when the owner's daughter arrived, brown
and gut-hurtingly beautiful in a shiny new car.
She waved to him and smiled, Sven was gone,
his blood sped in his veins, and he knew
she'd come no nearer to him ever in his life.

Young

■ *Anne Sexton*

A thousand doors ago
when I was a lonely kid
in a big house with four
garages and it was summer
as long as I could remember,
I lay on the lawn at night,

clover wrinkling under me,
the wise stars bedding over me,
my mother's window a funnel
of yellow heat running out,
my father's window, half shut,
an eye where sleepers pass,
and the boards of the house
were smooth and white as wax
and probably a million leaves
sailed on their strange stalks
as the crickets ticked together
and I, in my brand-new body,
which was not a woman's yet,
told the stars my questions
and thought God could really see
the heat and the painted light,
elbows, knees, dreams, goodnight.

Gaining Yardage

■ *Leo Dangel*

The word *friend* never came up
between Arlo and me—we're farm neighbors
who hang around together, walk beans,
pick rocks, and sit on the bench
at football games, weighing the assets
of the other side's cheerleaders.
Tonight we lead 48 to 6, so the coach
figures sending us both in is safe.
I intercept an underthrown pass
only because I'm playing the wrong position,
and Arlo is right there to block for me
because he's in the wrong place,
so we gallop up the field, in the clear
until their second-string quarterback
meets us at the five-yard line,
determined to make up for his bad throw.
Arlo misses the block, the guy has me
by the leg and jersey, and going down,
I flip the ball back to Arlo, getting up,
who fumbles, and their quarterback
almost recovers, then bobbles the ball
across the goal line, and our coach,
who told even the guys with good hands
never to mess around with laterals,
must feel his head exploding,
when Arlo and I dive on the ball together
in the end zone and dance and slap
each other on the back.
They give Arlo the touchdown, which rightly
should be mine, but I don't mind,
and I suppose we are friends, and will be,
unless my old man or his decides to move
to another part of the country.

Target Practice

■ *Gary Soto*

When we fired our rifles
We spooked sparrows from the tree.
Bottles burst when we aimed.
Tin cans did more than *ping*
And throw themselves in dry grass.
The dog pulled in tail and ears,
Saddened his eyes and crawled under the car.
We smiled at this, Leonard and I,
And went to look at the tin cans
And push our fingers into the holes—
Pink worms wagging at our happiness.
We set them up again, blew jagged zeros
On all sides, and then sat down
To eat sandwiches, talk about girls,
School, and how to get by on five-dollar dates.
Finished eating, we called the dog
With finger snaps and tongue clicks,
But he crawled deeper into shadow.
We searched the car trunk for Coke cans,
Found three, and set them further away.
We raised the rifles, winced an eye,
And fired, Leonard hitting
On the third try, me on the fifth.
We jumped up and down, laughed, and waved
A hand through the drifts of gun smoke,
Then the two of us returned to the car
Where we dragged the dog into the backseat.
We started the engine, let it idle in smoke,
And raised our rifles one last time,
The grass and dirt leaping into air.
We laughed and took a step back,
Packed the rifles in oily blankets,
And revved the engine. We turned onto the road
Without a good thought in our heads,
Ready for life.

Muscling Rocks

■ *Robert Morgan*

Back in times too poor
to target-waste our ammunition
all the boys and young men
would wander out in Henry's pasture
on Sunday afternoons
to lift the harvest of rocks.
Anyone could start by loosening
a big one from its pocket
in the hillside and chesting it,
then straining,
sometimes with a fart,
to press it overhead.
Dropped, it made a new dent
in the clover.
All who challenged
had to lift in turn.
There was no order,
no successive difficulty. One
wrestled out whatever stone
he fancied and could jerk,
or staggered back and let
it roll away toward the creek.
Sometimes the older raised one
with a cowpile on one side
and the young would smear it on
their chins before noticing.
Or the final sport would be
to piss on someone's leg
while he was busy heaving.
That usually made things end
with one good fight.

Hank and Peg

■ *William Burt*

He was as skinny
As I was
But wiry
The kid next door
Who was everything
Summer was made of
White T-shirt
Freckles
An ugly crew cut
An uglier dog
A red bike
Without fenders
His name was Hank
Together
We cultivated boredom
As though it were
A rare orchid
In the shade
Of the carport
Beside the fallout shelter
Beside the house
Where his family lived
The pavement there
Cool to the touch
Was a hotbed
Of get-rich-quick schemes
And Charles Atlas ads
Experiments with firecrackers
That didn't go off
On the Fourth
And still didn't go off
On the twenty-fourth
Experiments in creative talking
Backwards
Who could talk the longest
The fastest
With water in your mouth

Warm hose water
Acting out the final scene
Of Bataan
Careful not to die
In the oil puddle
Acting out
Godzilla Meets Werewolf
While the sun
Not even moving
An inch
Baked front yards
And gnats crawled the lips
Of the ugly dog sleeping
Her name was Peg
And she was old
Before there were
People on the earth
There was Peg
Toothless
Panting
We thought she was smiling
It was canine air-conditioning
We thought she was a bulldog
She was a Boston terrier
Ugly, bloated, unafraid
Even of death
Which was on her
Like a smell
Bored enough to provoke Peg
We would grab at her club feet
And make fun
Of old Peg
Old blind Peg
Old fat Peg
Until a death-rattle snarl
Became a neckless lurch
Peg gummed the air
And sometimes
An inch of finger
Reminded her
Of the taste

Of sweeter days
Peg the fighter
Triumphant
Cat killer
The world
May not remember
But the heart
Never forgets
And so it is
That I recall
Mississippi summers
And a carport
And the sound of a screen door
An aimless whistled tune
I would look out the window
There was Hank
Coming through the hedge
Peg at his heel
And the day would begin

Eagle Rock

■ *Geof Hewitt*

Remember us to Eagle Rock
Billy Koenig & me at 9 years apiece
hiking one Saturday in early May
way up past the house with half a pack
of embezzled cigarettes & enough matches
to light each one a dozen times,

Remember us to Eagle Rock
where couples in their cars
pulled off the road to watch the N.Y. skyline
& make love as Billy & me
dizzy from tobacco sitting on the big pavilion
of the castle with its stoned-out windows
wondering what to do once we felt better

And how as if we had no choice
we'd find ourselves each time
working toward the place the cars were parked
provided by the town, a pressure seal
for lovers prevented by circumstance
from doing it at home

And picture Koenig & me, pockets stuffed
with newly sprouted acorns
we used to stone the lovers
I can't believe we stoned the lovers
taking such liberties with our health
& how, when we did get chased

we'd run & run & run
half laughing & half very scared
some wild-yelling cursing half-dressed
passion victim in pursuit
I hated to trip but often did
Billy usually way ahead of me, down down
into the forest below Eagle Rock
to a cave we knew where
we'd heave & choke & get our breath,
lungs aching from the cigarettes & from the chase
& laugh & swear we'd never come so close
to getting caught

Swinging the River

■ *Charles Harper Webb*

One by one they climbed out on the thickest limb,
crouched like 12-year-old Tarzans, then
jumped, whipped through needley branches,
strangling the hemp rope till their nerve broke
and they dropped thirty feet to the river.

I was second-to-last in line. Second-
to-chickenest, I guessed. I'd never done this.

Rocks and tricky currents had drowned two kids
in three years. (One was never found.)
My mother'd kill me if she knew. . . .

My turn. My shaking hands grabbed at the rope.
I didn't dare think, just jumped,
swooped down, arced up, higher, flew free,
seemed to hang in the air while the splash
reached up to swallow me, blacking out

the sun, the feathery pine trees,
the blonde girl on the bank
whose wet shirt showed her swelling nipples,
who'd said hi the day before,
who was here with her aunt for two short weeks.

I sank like an anvil. Colder and colder.
I quietly gave up hope. Then my feet
touched a dead kid. Slime-hands
clutched at me. I kicked wildly
into sickening ooze, broke free, went shooting up

through millions of bubbles, rocketing out
into the blonde girl's smile.

Jump

■ *Jo Carson*

Jay said I was yellow
if I didn't and chose
a place toward the middle
of Pickens Bridge where
I would not touch bottom,
said it was dangerous
with stumps and barbed wire
that had been flooded.
I stood on the railing,
filled my lungs again,
and stepped into the air.

Downlake, I saw a skier
launch and fall,
children eating drumsticks,
a man moving in his boat.
I saw the water, green,
rising and shut my eyes,
held my nose two-fisted

and plunged in with fish.
The soles of my feet stung.
Water lifted my elbows,
spread my legs and toes,
turned me some easier way.
I knew deep water,
knew it from the tub
when I ran my bath
to overflowing, knew it
from the deep end
of a swimming pool
when I dived to touch
the painted TWELVE.
I knew to swim for light
but there was no light.
Soundings made, deep
and urgent in my ears.
Older, colder places
waited and I passed
through them with no end
left to imagine but a first
easy breath of water.
When I felt the mud
packed hard into the bed
of the river that still
runs inside Boone Lake,
I jumped, a pink frog
who learned UP, and rose

and broke at the surface,
come a second time to air.

Their Names

Scrawny   Bumper   Zip
names more alive
than parents' labels:
Lawrence   Russell   Marvin

terms to cringe at
chosen for reflected fame
or family pride
affixed like talismans:
George   Stanley   Albert

Deke   Magoo   Fet
handles casually acquired
from playgrounds and poolhalls
the namers now unknown
the occasions obscure

names taboo to teachers
sure to repel parents
earned by them
conferred by them

their names

Preposterous

■ *Jim Hall*

At fifteen Jean Calvin made a list:
Best Legs, Sexiest Smile, Best Muscles,
all the rest. She had the right to judge us
since she was Most Buxom herself,
Most Dreamed About,
Most Discussed When Flesh Came Up.

I sat behind her in Civics that aromatic year
and whispered jokes and tried to breathe her hair.
For all that I won Wittiest. Wittiest.
And was runner-up for Best Legs on a Short Boy.

She posted it and overnight her picks
for All-round Sexiest, Perkiest Buns, Dreamiest,
drew flocks around their lockers.
And everything I said was suddenly preposterous
and clever. I could roll my eyes that June
and break up Biology.

It wasn't what I wanted, but I took it.
I wanted to be one of those who could whisper
in Jean Calvin's hair and make her wheel and slap
and turn back around with a secret smile.
I wanted a gift: Best Voice, Bedroomiest Eyes,
some arousing inherited trait. Not this,
this Wittiest, which makes me work so hard,
so everlastingly, to keep Jean Calvin entertained.

Every Chance We Got

■ *Charles Harper Webb*

Bob, Ted, and I (13 apiece) would take off hunting.
Rifles carried proud as our new body hair,
we'd tramp for hours with little kill
and less concern, until we felt like stopping
to rest, or take a leak, or listen
to some scurrying in the gray-brown brush.

Dusk would be holding night barely at bay.
Our faces would be redder than our hunting caps (almost),
our coats as warm as winter blankets home in bed.
We'd find a fallen tree, or clearing rusted over
with pine needles, and sit, legs tingling from walking,
voices steaming in the autumn air.

Then, like a coal carried faithfully all day,
someone would bring up "girls," and talk would flare.
Girls: soft; giggly; their presence bright
as sun on open water. Girls: their mystery
darker, wilder even than the woods. Then on
to summer jobs, sports, great careers—money
and how rich we'd be someday, when we'd do everything. . . .

Maybe we never quite believed
in those naked girls on yachts on sky-blue seas,
those batting crowns and XKEs and glorious TV lives.
But we could almost clutch them, Bardot-like,
into life with picturing—until, night closing in,
someone remembered dinner; and we stomped back
like strapping ghosts, laughing all the fading way home.

Boys' Night Out

■ *Mark Vinz*

That's what we named it—
Fridays at the Folly Theater downtown,
the last of the burlesque houses,
which leaked its grimy stuffing
to the band's arthritic lurch,
where old men down in front
called out to each tired beauty
bumping through the tinted glow.
Once by mistake the house lights
came on bright
and we forever knew
what naked really means—
and told each other
how we'd never come again,
went home
to dream of winning teams
and warm beer gulped in cold backseats.
But still they danced, they danced—
the hot, damp pulse of boyhood
held us, told us
we'd be back.

during the sermon . . .

■ *William Kloefkorn*

during the sermon
ludi jr dreams of the girl
in the next pew

how her long blonde hair
must follow her
everywhere

when she sits down
the hair settling itself in place
not daring to move
until spoken to

when she enters the dime store
the hair reaching out and down
to examine the cold cream

in potter's grocery
the hair polishing the apples
catching their fire

and at night

oh at night!

the tip ends sparking the linen

Juke Box Love Song

■ *Langston Hughes*

I could take the Harlem night
and wrap around you,
Take the neon lights and make a crown,
Take the Lenox Avenue buses,
Taxis, subways,
And for your love song tone their rumble down.
Take Harlem's heartbeat,
Make a drumbeat,
Put it on a record, let it whirl,
And while we listen to it play,
Dance with you till day—
Dance with you, my sweet brown Harlem girl.

Matinees

■ *Katherine Soniat*

By twos we flocked
to the Mecca movie matinee,
growing breathless over the word "censored."
Fuchsia-lipped and solemn,
we aged our way into *The Moon Is Blue*
and felt our hearts' collective thump

as the redhead mouthed the culprit
word "seduce." In the dark
we straightened with a nudge,
forgetting that summer of huddles
in the lightning-hollowed oak.
There, staring up that charred alley

to the sky, we vowed,
"I would never do *that*. Even with my brother."
And we scurried from the tree and on
to our hideout
in leafy summer bush to glimpse
the neighborhood weight lifter

in his loose-legged shorts.
At four-thirty his dumbbells clanged
through the open garage window,
the work whistle shrilled for evening
from the old molasses factory,
its dark vats coating the air we breathed.

The Love Nest

■ *Leo Dangel*

Well I don't care, Denise,
if you didn't win
the Dairy Princess Pageant.

By the time we're married
next spring, the new house
on the farm will be finished,
with a double garage
for your car and my pickup.
We'll panel the basement
with walnut veneer or maple
and tear down the old house
when my old man moves to town.
There'll be a new steel barn
and another Harvestore silo.
You know as well as I do,
Denise, you could hardly ask
for a better deal.
You're beautiful, Denise,
and I think if I bit
into your shoulder right now,
you'd taste like watermelon.

Howie Kell Suspends All Lust to Contemplate the Universe

■ *Rodney Torreson*

I'm for creationism, not the big bang,
then Valerie Marslott, in a friendly tank top,
cousin of Dad's army buddy's children,
visits our farm. Valerie has me rub up
behind her, teaches me to show her how
to swing a bat. Later,
while Mom makes sundaes, she,
who I'd met an hour before, sits on my lap.
She wants us to eat from the same dish,
lick the same spoon, as if life
arose from some primordial soup,
then evolved through a series of accidents.
Oh Valerie, will my mom's prayers save you?
There's order in her table setting,

in Dad's bringing in a folding chair.
I still believe in the clay-life theory, yes,
though it would be shaken by your milky kiss.

Cheerleader

■ *Jim Wayne Miller*

Seventeen and countless times French-kissed,
her body marbled milk and honey, bread
and wine on tongues at halftime Eucharist,
she takes the floor to be distributed.

Jammed bleachers all at once are smitten dumb.
Deliciously she sways; her metered cheers
ricochet off girders in the gym;
they fall like sibyls' leaves over the tiers.

She spins; her skirt, gathering speed, whirls,
floats off her dimpled knees slender thighs
snug red panties—stands, falls.
The sweating crowd speaks tongues and prophecies.

Fat Girl with Baton

■ *Bob Henry Baber*

She cheerleads a team
of junior weight watchers,

promises orange Popsicle prizes
for The Perfect Cartwheel
& Impossible Split

already the vogue ways of the world
are fixed against her baby fat breasts

Still she spins her baton
with heart-pink faith,

poises
to toss her chromatic hopes
into the metallic sky—

her leopard leotard
like first love
stretched beyond redemption

her Majorette Dreams
as predestined as oak leaves
to meet the ground

untouched

For People Who Can't Open Their Hoods

■ *Jim Daniels*

Some fat lady in a mink
storms in
says her car won't start
left her lights on
got her son outside with cables
but they don't know how
to open the hood.

Because I'm head stockboy
because she's a good customer
they send me out to help her.
I grin at the two of them
son fat as mother
shaking pink cheeks in the cold
cables dangling from his gloved hands.
He hands them to me
like they're dead snakes.

I pop open the hood
of the mother's new Grand Prix.
They stand aside yapping
not even looking at me.
I start up the son's Cadillac
and sit behind the wheel for a while.
They look at the mother's packages
that I carried out minutes before
without getting a tip.

I rev it up, my foot to the floor
while I check out the plush interior
stereo tape deck, digital clock, cruise control
power everything.
I beep the horn.
They stand in the cold
suddenly looking at me.

I put the car in reverse
and back out to move in position
for the jump.
I put it in drive and grip the wheel
and for one long moment
they think   I think
I will drive away.

Of Necessity,
Weeb Jokes About His Height

■ *Charles Harper Webb*

I was going great till tenth grade:
four-eleven to nearly five-foot-seven in three years.
I strode around in a brawny six-foot air shell
like a twelve-year-old, 32A girl who buys
a 38D bra for the fun of watching it fill.
Then, like a cake dropped
from five-feet-six-and-three-fourths inches up,
my growth abruptly stopped, and spoiled the party.

My twice-daily measurings and desperate wishes
brought me no nearer the five-eight "average" mark
I'd scratched contemptuously on my bedroom door—
a pit stop, a mere first camp on my way up.
None of my stretching exercises,
my elaborately planned, constantly revised diets
would squeeze out one more micron.

I'd heard of "the power of positive thinking";
I thought positive. I'd heard
"A watched pot never boils." I cut out measuring
for weeks, sneaking peeks at the five-eight mark,
sure it was eye level. I apologized to God
for doubting Him, and prayed fervently, just in case.
I devoured books on adolescence, reading and rereading
(along with the parts on sex) the part which said
some men had growth spurts until twenty-one.

But truth, like skunk scent on a thousand-dollar suit,
sunk in.
Dad was short and burly; Mother, tall and slim.
I would be short and thin.
No Mickey Mantle. No Johnny Unitas.
No Wilt Chamberlain, Rocky Marciano, Big John Wayne.

I would never hit 60 homers, gain 1,000 yards,
sink 50 points a game. I'd never stretch
a loudmouth out cold with one careless swipe
of my huge right hand. Brigitte Bardot,
Racquel Welch, would not be mine.

I would slink through gym afraid of hoods,
have drab girlfriends, and lose them to tall men.
I would flirt with karate and weight lifting,
learn to play guitar, join a rock-and-roll band.
I would become an intellectual.

Poetry Lesson Number One

■ *Wanda Coleman*

Cleveland and them hung out in that Watts café used
   to be
   across the
tracks on a diagonal north of the workshop off 103rd. No
   women were
allowed at that table unless being schemed upon, or of
   exceptional beauty.
But I was a stubborn little mud hen at the fringe of
   the clique,
   starved
for approval.

So one day Cleveland and them was sitting at the table.
   Cleve
   and maybe
Eric and one other brother. I boldly intruded on their
   exclusivity with
my neat little sheaf of poems.

"And so you write?" and "Let us see one!" And the
   other
   brother took it and
read it out loud and they passed it around the table.

"Hmmmm" and "Ahhhh."
And I blushed and my stomach tightened twice for each of my
19 years.

"Oh yeeeaahhh," said Cleveland. "You are a writer,
   young
   lady. As good a
writer as a man!"

And I caught the bus home, carrying his words with me,
   clutching my thin
little poems to my heart,

glowing in the dark.

Mrs. Krikorian

■ *Sharon Olds*

Today I remembered Mrs. Krikorian,
how she saved my bacon. I arrived in sixth grade
a known criminal, and the new teacher
asked me to stay after school the first day, she said
I've heard about you.
She was a tall woman, deep-breasted, with a
mass of dark hair around her face
and a large, calm nose. She said
You see this? It was a little card,
small white card that saved me from evil,
This is a special library pass.
As soon as you finish the hour's work—that
hour's work that took ten minutes and
then the devil glanced into the room and
found me empty, a house standing open, FOR
RENT, FOR SALE, FIRE SALE, FIRE—
you can go to the library. Hour after hour I'd
zip through the work and slip out of my
seat like an angel out of God's side and sail

down to the library, down through the empty
powerful halls, flash my pass and
sashay over to the dictionary to
look up *spank*, dipping two fingers
into the vat of library paste to
suck that minty mucilage while I
came to the page with the cocker spaniel's
silks curling up like the fine steam of the body.
After *spank* and *breast* I'd move on to
Abe Lincoln and *Helen Keller*,
lost in goodness till the bell—all thanks to
Mrs. Krikorian, amiable giantess
with the brown eyes. Next she asked me to
write a Christmas play and direct it, and
when it was imperfect and I hid in the closet came
up to me in the coaty rubbery
dark and held out a tiny cane of
scarlet and milk-white peppermint as you
lay a candy on the tongue of a child and the
worm will come up out of the bowel to get it.
And so I was emptied of Lucifer and
filled with school glue and eros and
Amelia Earhart, saved by Mrs. Krikorian.
Today for the first time I saw:
Mrs. Krikorian was Armenian. And then:
who saved Mrs. Krikorian?
When the Turks came across the fields like a thresher
flailing its blades, who slid her
into the slit belly of a quilt, who
locked her in a chest, who mailed her to America?
And that one, who saved her, when the Turks
came with their thumpers, their rat-hunt clubs,
and that one,
who saved her to save the one who
saved Mrs. Krikorian who was
standing there on the sill of sixth grade like a
wide-hipped angel, aura of smoky
hair standing up lightly all around her head?
I end up owing my soul to so many,
to the Armenian nation, one more soul someone
jammed behind a stove, drove

deep into the crack of a wall,
shoved under a bed. I remember
lying there, under the bed
in the dusk, the dust balls at my head and feet
round and silver, shining slightly with the
eerie sweetness of what is neither good nor evil.

Sister

■ *Mike Lowery*

you said red hair made you
different. in the
alchemy of memory I still
see two clocks lost
wanderers fumbling for
lucky strikes behind
Whitner's dry goods store.
losing track of time in our
search for magicians and poets

I danced in iron
shoes—ah but
you, on the edge of
the fire pit, lit by
the flames of the jukebox, danced
in the wild heart of the fire.

till, with a baby in
your belly, you became
a fearful bird, ever
hearing the hawk's bell.

Trouble

■ *James Wright*

*Well, look, honey, where I come from, when a girl says
she's in trouble, she's in trouble.*—JUDY HOLLIDAY

Leering across Pearl Street,
Crum Anderson yipped:
"Hey Pugh!
I see your sister
Been rid bareback.

She swallow a watermelon?
Fred Gordon! Fred Gordon! Fred Gordon!"
"Wayya mean? She can get fat, can't she?"

Fat? Willow and lonesome Roberta, running
Alone down Pearl Street in the rain the last time
I ever saw her, smiling a smile
Crum Anderson will never know,
Wondering at her body.

Sixteen years, and
All that time she thought she was nothing
But skin and bones.

Sister

■ *H. R. Coursen*

Younger than they,
and not the same.
Girl growing amid
a grove of brothers.
They took my dolls
one day into their
forbidden circle
in the woods,
drove sticks
into the cleared dirt,
and burned them
at the stake.

Evening Dawn

■ *Herbert Scott*

I remember an evening on the farm,
my sisters and I on the lawn after rain,
young foxes in a green pasture,
the sun gone behind miles of clouds
and the western sky black;

yet a strange green light over all,
crickets sounding in the trees,
leaves like tongues spilling wetness,
the damp breath of their singing;

and my sisters and I on the lawn
listening to quail calling,
the evening holding light like the sea,
the sun lost in the deeps of the sky;

yet as if by miracle
a light coming from the east,
from a clear sky beyond massed clouds:
an evening dawn, sending shadows westward;

and we stood in that luminous gift,
in that moment out of order
as if the earth had turned a strange orbit,
our lives long shadows before us.

The moment soon gone, we moved to the sound
of whippoorwills, the odor of lilac,
the tongues of the trees sifting hymns.

■ *Eric Trethewey*

I

Sunday, beginning the week late,
I roust him from his sour dreams
to cut firewood. At the top of the sky,
clear-edged through fog, a pale sun
hangs above our labor as we do
what we can with a dull saw,
our lungs full of December.
My brother, not yet eighteen,
has flown south out of the old life
ready to learn how to break
the past's twisting drag. He's serious,
works hard on his side of the horse,
until the blade begins to bow and bind
in the oak, and I tell him not to force it,
to hold the saw easy, draw lightly
across the cut, let the tool do the work.
And though he listens, begins to learn,
beyond this small matter between us
he hears nothing of what I say,
says he wants to know where to score
some weed in this new place.
How to keep him out of jail is what I want
to know, and keep his fists in his pockets
through one more year of school,
make him see that we're all dull blades
ready to slant and bind in twisted cuts.

II

Late afternoon, at the Laundromat,
cold drizzle misting around us,
we wait for the last load to dry.
Having offered him all-day advice
he hasn't heard, I slump in the car, reading
while he prowls the puddled lot
looking for what I can't imagine,

thin and bitter under his worn clothes,
two thousand miles from home,
my young brother adrift in his life.
Looking up from my book, I see him stoop,
pick up something from the gravel
that he brings toward me, hand extended.
"It's the smallest frog I've ever seen,"
he says, astonished, and carries it out,
gently, toward the green and dripping trees.

Wheels

■ *Jim Daniels*

My brother kept
in a frame on the wall
pictures of every motorcycle, car, truck:
in his rusted out Impala convertible
wearing his cap and gown
waving
in his yellow Barracuda
with a girl leaning into him
waving
on his Honda 350
waving
on his Honda 750 with the boys
holding a beer
waving
in his first rig
wearing a baseball hat backwards
waving
in his Mercury Montego
getting married
waving
in his black LTD
trying to sell real estate
waving
back to driving trucks
a shiny new rig

waving
on his Harley Sportster
with his wife on the back
waving
his son in a car seat
with his own steering wheel
my brother leaning over him
in an old Ford pickup
and they are
waving
holding a wrench a rag
a hose a shammy
waving.

My brother helmetless
rides off on his Harley
waving
my brother's feet
rarely touch the ground—
waving waving
face pressed to the wind
no camera to save him.

The Winter They Bombed Pearl Harbor

■ *Walter McDonald*

The winter they bombed Pearl Harbor,
my brother finally let me follow
up the deepest snowdrift in the town.
Each blizzard whipped between two homes

and piled dead-end on Joe Hall's shed,
long and low as a bunkhouse. Drifts
seemed like hills on plains so flat
I'd never seen a sled. In weeks,

my brother was off for war, and he dragged
and carried me up to the roof of the world.
Holding me high by one hand, he dropped me
like a flag up to my crotch in snow so soft

I believed if he let me go I'd sink.
There must have been something else
we did up there, Ed and his friends and me
the tagalong. But even if he let me fall

and had to tunnel down to save me,
if I sank, I can't recall. I've stared
and stared at these four pictures of us
like climbers, but nothing clicks. I'd like

to think I understood where he was going,
what war was and risk, and what
a brother meant. Even now, I try
to feel that afternoon, reach down my feet

on something solid I remember and hold
it all and turn it over like a snowball
in my mind, now that I'm old enough to value
loss, but I can't bring my brother back.

Smoke

■ *Eric Pankey*

My brother and I cut a tunnel
into a border of flowerless
rosebushes that separated
one square rutted field from another.

At dusk, in the hollow we had cut,
the thorn branches tangled above us
—a clumsy loosening weave
of the jay's nest tumbled by wind.

Last light fell in pale scribblings
upon our hands and faces as we worked.
And we worked hard. The place was our own.
My brother hid his trinkets

in a hole we'd dug in the red clay floor:
the skull of a robin rubbed smooth by rain,
matches, steel pennies from 1943,
and fossils—*sea grass* he told me

from when the whole plain was covered
with ocean. He knew about such things.
Once, we risked a fire of twigs and dried leaves.
As it burned, I added strands of green vine

and damp greasy smoke filled the hedge.
At least a hundred granddaddy longlegs
fell into our hair, and around us,
and those that fell into the fire

gave off a sickening smell of sulfur.
We were sure it was some sort of magic.
The fire moved up the arc of limbs.
The rain of spiders would not stop.

By then, our father was calling us in, but
we could not see the porch light, or
his figure black against the screen door.
We knew we were in for it now.

Smoke spread through the tunnel. The dark
was close enough to fill the cracks.

Zimmer in Grade School

■ *Paul Zimmer*

In grade school I wondered
Why I had been born
To wrestle in the ashy puddles,
With my square nose
Streaming mucus and blood,
My knuckles puffed from combat
And the old nun's ruler.
I feared everything: God,
Learning and my schoolmates.
I could not count, spell or read.
My report card proclaimed
These scarlet failures.
My parents wrung their loving hands.
My guardian angel wept constantly.

But I could never hide anything.
If I peed my pants in class
The puddle was always quickly evident,
My worst mistakes were at
The blackboard for Jesus and all
The saints to see.

Even now
When I hide behind elaborate masks
It is always known that I am Zimmer,
The one who does the messy papers
And fractures all his crayons,
Who spits upon the radiators
And sits all day in shame
Outside the office of the principal.

The Mad Nun

■ *Dana Gioia*

for Alexander Theroux

The convent yard seems larger than before
  when late last night he stood a moment
    on Paul's unsteady shoulders

and saw a garden in the moonlight
  full of flower beds and orange trees
    around a green-rimmed, empty pond.

Now the paths extend for miles, disappearing
  only in the gloom of trees
    that run along a wall of hedges.

At first the dreamer travels with
  his classmates, but one
    by one they drop away. Paul

transformed into a rosebush when he trips
  on a gardener's shovel. James
    sinks unresistingly into the green

surface of the pond and swims away
  a goldfish. Ernie, whose
    mother warned him when he swore,

steps off the gravel path and blends
  into the ivy, sobbing
    as his hair grows

long and green curling up a tree,
  and slowly the survivor realizes
    that everything growing in this garden

was once a schoolboy—the battered statues,
  the drooping trees, the quiet
    vines climbing up the wall.

Even the spider suspended at the entrance
  of the arbor sits trapped
    like a housefly on his web.

"How do I get out of here?"
  he begs the statues near the pond
    who cannot leave their perpetual

transfixion: Francis in ecstasy
  among the duckweed and beatific
    Dominic who smiles at the birdbath.

But it is always too late.
  A horrible laugh comes
    from behind the Grotto of Our Lady,

and then he knows that the mad nun
  everyone hears about
    has seen him in the garden.

He scrambles down the path, hearing
  her heavy, square-toed shoes
    scuff the ground behind him,

and runs between the hedges—until,
  hidden in the oleander, he hears nothing
    but his own heart beating from exertion

and thinks he has lost her. But suddenly
  he sees a flash of black
    and white behind the bushes.

There is never time to run away
  before her long, white hands
    reach out and shake him

awake, shivering in a damp bed,
  listening to the rain
    drive nails into the roof,

waiting hours
  for the humiliating
    light of dawn.

The Purpose of Altar Boys

■ *Alberto Rios*

Tonio told me at catechism
the big part of the eye
admits good, and the little
black part is for seeing
evil—his mother told him,
who was a widow and so
an authority on such things.
That's why at night
the black part gets bigger.
That's why kids can't go out
at night, and at night
girls take off their clothes
and walk around their
bedrooms or jump on their
beds or wear only sandals
and stand in their windows.
I was the altar boy
who knew about these things,
whose mission on some Sundays
was to remind people of
the night before as they
knelt for Holy Communion.
To keep Christ from falling
I held the metal plate
under chins, while on the thick
red carpet of the altar
I dragged my feet
and waited for the precise
moment: plate to chin
I delivered without expression
the Holy Electric Shock,
the kind that produces
a really large swallowing
and makes people think.
I thought of it as justice.
But on other Sundays the fire
in my eyes was different,

my mission somehow changed.
I would hold the metal plate
a little too hard
against those certain same
nervous chins, and I
I would look
with authority down
the tops of white dresses.

Music Lessons

■ *Judith Volmer*

My mother packed me off to music school in May
and the college girls wore white gloves.
Sister Ann Agnes said:
"No, don't look at *me*. Don't look at your hands.
Close your eyes. Listen and you'll hear it."
She sang a high, bird note. I listened,
my eyes gliding over light pools on the wall.
Notes were everywhere,
secret as the girls' voices out on the lawn.
I found high F sharp. She smiled,
giving me the first perfect thing
I'd ever known.

Now she sang her mellowest note,
its tremolo breathing across the top of my hair.
She leaned toward the open window
and the vibrato curled into my spine.
I watched sprinklers wave
like silver harps. I played
a simplified Debussy,
my fingers skinny birds over water,
the water rising
like mist above the keys.

The Strand Theatre

■ *Teresa Cader*

Lovesick girls, old men in foul underwear
inhabit this movie theatre
in Trenton, New Jersey, in the fifties,
before the riots, before debutantes
are murdered in their town houses.
The most beautiful man we have ever seen
is making love to a woman we envy.
She lifts her thigh, we are breathless.
When they are not making love,
she cries, he drives his Ferrari
to an empty beach where he paces
the cliffs, imagining how he will leave
his wife. She waits in a back room,
as if she would wait there her whole life,
until one night coming to see her,
he crashes the Ferrari into a parked truck,
dies in her arms. We sob, lurching
in our seats. Old men yell at us
from the balcony, only I can't stop,
neither can you. You make syncopated snorts,
I hiccup as if on a megaphone.
Then you whisper *we sound like toads*,
and we are laughing, bleating like little goats
through the funeral all the way to the cemetery,
and God knows what has happened to the woman
whose man just died, because we are ushered
from the theatre, returned to the street,
where on the littered sidewalk
we stand astonished and thirteen.

The Time We Cherry-Bombed the Toilet at the River Oaks

■ *Charles Harper Webb*

I stood guard outside the scarred stall
as Randy lit the fuse. I heard it
fizzing like an Alka Seltzer, then
the flush, the toilet's roar as we
rushed for the door, the blast, a deep

belch, a sonic boom heard with a pillow
on your head. I pictured the white
"throne" cracking like a fossil egg,
a thousand-legged water monster leaping
out to get us as we fled,

flattening a little kid standing
alone in red-striped shorts, his popcorn
spraying up into the air, his howls
and brays mixing with the ushers'
pounding feet and hisses. Their flash-

lights slashed through the dim room
where a crowd of kids fidgeted and fought
through on-screen kisses. Hurling jujubes
and chewed gum, they screamed for a gunfight,
Indian attack, anything besides a man

and woman trading drool, as Randy and I,
feeling adult and cool, slipped into
empty seats and, for the first time,
not screaming with the others, settled
into the dark's soft, inviting arms.

Autobiographical Note

■ *Vernon Scannell*

Beeston, the place, near Nottingham:
We lived there for three years or so.
Each Saturday at two o'clock
We queued up for the matinee.
All the kids for streets around
With snotty noses, giant caps,
Cut down coats and heavy boots,
The natural enemies of cops
And schoolteachers. Profane and hoarse
We scrambled, yelled and fought until
The Picture Palace opened up
And we, like Hamelin children, forced
Our bony way into the hall.
That much is easy to recall;
Also the reek of chewing gum,
Gob-stoppers and licorice,
But of the flickering myths themselves
Not much remains. The hero was
A milky wide-brimmed hat, a shape
Astride the arched white stallion;
The villain's horse and hat were black.
Disbelief did not exist
And laundered virtue always won
With quicker gun and harder fist,
And all of us applauded it.
Yet I remember moments when
In solitude I'd find myself
Brooding on the sooty man,
The bristling villain, who could move
Imagination in a way
The well-shaved hero never could,
And even warm the nervous heart
With something oddly close to love.

Shaking

■ *Robert Morgan*

For us a handshake was a duel:
two boys in a friendly clasp
of greeting were fighting a test
of power. Who squeezed first might have
an advantage, unless the cold
tendons got strained, and the grip,
so big and cruel, at once would
weaken from the quick exertion
as the other built up a grasp
that overrode and then melted
the opposing hand, while we both
kept grinning hello. But the best
defense was to cup your palm so
knuckles weren't aligned for grinding
but curled under the hostile force.
It was the feint of giving in,
while the rival bore down and thought
himself near victory, that was
the last strategy. And when he
crunched you toward acquiescence and
withdrawal from the lethal shake,
you put everything, your whole weight
and blood and warmth and thought, pumped down
through wrist and elbow and shoulder
on the opponent's paw as his
smile registered surprise and pain
and you broke down his control in
the vise of your own gesture of
reciprocation, serious welcome.

Jody Walker: The First Voice

■ *Paul Ruffin*

Jody—the name conjures fawn and fowl,
the smack of scuppernong wine.

Strung in a row, we lolled each
morning, waiting for his bus
to reach school, our tongues
and fingers sharp to touch
what he delivered: blackberries
silver with dew and big as cows' eyes,
possum on a chain, rat snake
around his neck, pickled
pig embryo, rubbers with spikes,
wines rendered from the wildest fruits,
the stuffed two-headed calf
John Parker threw up over,
owl eggs, flying squirrels,
dried bull balls black as coal—
his store of exotics as endless
as the earth itself.

Shorter by a head than most of us,
he had merely to wink, gesture,
cup a palm toward us and we
followed, older, younger, where he led.

He charmed us with tales
of coupling animals, showed us
how babies came to be, shared
photographs of nudes, taught us
how farm boys drove deep
into the soft of fruit and beasts.

His was our brightest sin:
Our dwarf god from out
as far as the buses could go
stepped down from his yellow
chariot, his hand beckoning.
His secrets burned in us;
each morning we grew in his flame
beneath the simple sun.

Walking with Jackie, Sitting with a Dog

■ *Gary Soto*

Jackie on the porch, shouting for me to come out.
It's Saturday, and I am in a sweater that's
Too large, balled at the elbows, black at the collar.
Laughing, we slam the screen door on a strained
Voice, and run down the street, sticks
In hand, shooing pigeons and the girls
Who are all legs.
                         We cross the gray traffic
Of Belmont, and enter an alley, its quick stream
Of glass blinking in the angled light. We blink,
And throw rocks at things that move,
Slow cat or bough. We grin
Like shovels, and continue on
Because it's Saturday, early as it's ever
Going to get, and we're brothers
To all that's heaved over fences.
Our talk is nonsense: Africa and trees splintered
Into matchsticks, handlebars and the widening targets
Of his sister's breasts, staring us down.
The scattered newspaper, cartwheeling across
A street, is one way to go.
                 And we go into
Another alley, where we find a man, asleep behind
Stacked cardboard. The sun flares
Behind trees and it means little.

We find a dog, hungry and sad as a suitcase kicked open
And showing nothing. At a curb we drape
Him across our laps and quarter an orange—
The juice runs like the tears an onion would give,
If only it opened its eye.
We lick our fingers and realize
That with oranges now and plums four months away,
No one need die.

The Antelope

■ *David Allan Evans*

When one of us hit
the deaf-and-dumb
junk dealer in the
back with a rock

the shiny
wooden handles of
his iron-wheeled
cart shot up
he whirled his
eye around and
screamed

the antelope in the scream

leaped out, had
nowhere to fly but
down the alley
our way and
just as we
took off it
blew through us
kicking up gravel
heading for
the Wall Street
viaduct on
electric legs.

A Brief Reversal: 1941

■ *Herbert Scott*

Merriman, you chased me home from school,
on your bicycle, long legs pumping, back humped,
face low and malevolent above the handlebars,
a fierce searchlight. No one liked you.
You were cruel in your stern disapproval
of the lack of suffering among the boys
at Miss Elder's school. Were we the enemy?

When you got polio, our school closed
for fumigation. Two weeks of unscheduled vacation!
But we were afraid. "This brings it close
to home," Miss Elder said. We should have filled
our March of Dimes cards that year with added vigor.
But, sorry to say, Merriman, you were not good
advertisement. For weeks I loitered home from school.
Our Dimes cards languised in our desks, half full.

We worked on special projects: presents
for you we made ourselves of spools and dowels,
then wrapped in colored tissue paper. One day,
late in March, our whole class walked to your house,
waited across the street, watching you
watch us from your bedroom window.
Miss Elder placed your presents on the porch
and rang the doorbell for your mother.

Well, Merriman, you recovered, returned
to school, meanness intact.
The March of Dimes also survived its brief reversal,
and, as you know, the rest is history.

Ronnie Schwinck

■ *David Allan Evans*

That day I squared off with
Ronnie Schwinck
in the alley behind
Woodrow Wilson Junior High,

he didn't look at me straight.

His look was like two
male dogs' eyes
when they meet and do
their cocked circles
around each other—
all you see,
all *I* saw, was the
unbelievably white edge
of Ronnie's stare.

That wild stare held us.

Nobody took a swing.

How It Was

■ *Gary Hyland*

Here's Scrawny toolin along
mull-too ta-too-too
mindin his own beeswax
when up comes this gearbox
with shoulders like yeh
and grabs him by the jacket
and says where's he goin
and Scrawny sees the biceps
this guy is packin
plus his three buddies

also heavily equipped
and says somethin like
up the street a ways
and the guy drops a juicer
right on Scrawny's shoe
So Scrawny tries walkin off
but the guy holds on tight
which is when Scrawny's knee
busts him in the eggs
and while the guy's down
stead of makin his break
Scrawny wipes the gob on him
That's when the others strike
The results you're gonna see
when we get up to his room
But remember—no funnies
He's got these wires in his jaw

No Question

■ *Leo Dangel*

There was no question,
I had to fight Arnold Gertz
behind the high school that Friday.
All fall he kept throwing pool balls
at me in the rec room.

There was no question,
I was scared spitless at the mere sight
of his grimy fists and bull neck.
When we rolled on the cinders
and grappled and thumped each other,

there was no question,
I was actually winning
when the principal broke us up.
And when Arnold went hunting pheasants
on Sunday, everybody said

there was no question,
he was a damn fool to climb through
a barbed wire fence with a loaded shotgun.
There were exactly eight of us guys
who were classmates of Arnold so

there was no question,
I had to be one of the pallbearers,
even though I never liked Arnold,
never would have, but I was sorry
the accident happened,

there was no question,
and if he hadn't got himself shot,
I wonder if he finally would have let me alone.
There is no question,
I wonder about that.

Gang Girls

■ *Gwendolyn Brooks*

Gang Girls are sweet exotics.
Mary Ann
uses the nutrients of her orient,
but sometimes sighs for Cities of blue and jewel
beyond her Ranger rim of Cottage Grove.
(Bowery Boys, Disciples, Whip-Birds will
dissolve no margins, stop no savory sanctities.)

Mary is
a rose in a whiskey glass.

Mary's
Februaries shudder and are gone. Aprils
fret frankly, lilac hurries on.
Summer is a hard irregular ridge.
October looks away.
And that's the Year!
            Save for her bugle-love.
Save for the bleat of not-obese devotion.

Save for Somebody Terribly Dying, under
the philanthropy of robins. Save for her Ranger
bringing
an amount of rainbow in a string-drawn bag.
"Where did you get the diamond?" Do not ask:
but swallow, straight, the spirals of his flask
and assist him at your zipper; pet his lips
and help him clutch you.

Love's another departure.
Will there be any arrivals, confirmations?
Will there be gleaning?

Mary, the Shakedancer's child
from the rooming-flat, pants carefully, peers at
her laboring lover. . . .
　　　　Mary! Mary Ann!
Settle for sandwiches! settle for stocking caps!
for sudden blood, aborted carnival,
the props and niceties of non-loneliness—
the rhymes of Leaning.

Sugar-n-Spice, etc.

■ *Rita Quillen*

All us girls knew about sin
sought after it.
Torn pieces of brown paper bags
wrapped around dried corn silks
secretly cured in the toolshed
supplied cigarettes to wave around
like those women on the soap operas.
In my friend's playhouse
we practiced kissing,
furtive and ashamed.
A high-powered telescope
Santa Claus brought
opened up the mysteries
of neighborhood bedrooms.

Once we sneaked out of a slumber party
tiptoed onto an icy bridge
still in our baby-doll pajamas,
froze our prissy asses off
to watch the sun stick out its tongue
at the gray world.
Then there was that Halloween
we rolled a septic tank
into the middle of the highway
and set it afire.

It took about 20 state troopers
two tow trucks and a tractor
to move that white-hot donut.
We were fairly disappointed
when nobody got arrested.
Our reputations weren't the best,

but at least what we were made of
wouldn't melt in your mouth.

Rites of Passage

■ *Dorianne Laux*

When we were sixteen, summer nights in the suburbs sizzled
like barbecue coals,
the hiss of lawn sprinklers,
telephone wires humming above our heads.
Sherry and me walked every block within five miles that year,
sneaking into backyards, peeking through windows,
we dared and double dared each other from behind the redwood slats.
Frog-legged, we slid down street lamps,
our laughter leaving trails of barking dogs behind us.
One night we came home the back way,
perfecting sexy walks and feeling "cool,"
and found my little sister on the side porch,
hiding behind the plastic trash bins in her nightgown,
smoking Salems,
making Monroe faces in a hand-held mirror.

Household

■ *Philip Booth*

This sad house.
Two girls gone.
The third girl

left, fifteen.
Three years to
go. Late from

staying after
school, she eats
alone with both

the same old
parents. Same
old meal: they

drink, she eats;
they eat, she
clears her plate.

Lead questions.
Moral mouth-
fuls. Between

them she grows
old, she tells
the same old

lies. Her sisters
have abandoned
her; she's wiser

than an only
child. She chokes
on what they

all three know,
meal after
meal: the house

is sad, it
cannot
hold.

News for the Cafeteria

■ *Sally Fisher*

News reached us in the high school cafeteria
that Darlene, the shapely one, who danced
to "The Breeze and I" in the sophomore show,
had eloped, on a school night, had climbed out
the window (left a note on the bed), and was gone.

How limber she must have been, in that one-
story ranch house, to roll through the narrow
horizontal window—up near the ceiling—
with a suitcase, and drop to the evergreen
shrubbery below. I never wondered then
why she hadn't used the door. To me,
perhaps to everyone in high school, out
the window was the only way to go.

The window was my best hope as long ago
as when I lowered my dolls on ropes to see
the view, or coaxed a trembling squirrel over
the sill, me as still as a Buddha with a
peanut. Or when I stared for hours into
the neighbor's guest room that never had a guest.
I was Rapunzel, longing for my great
release, impossible downstairs, through the door.

Even now I use the window when I can,
dropping down to city streets as if
it were water I moved in, and I lived
in a boat, and buildings and stores were coral reefs
waiting to be explored. I rise in the last
dark, press my palms through the yielding glass
and joining the predawn breeze I take my flight.
Sometimes, I turn back and see my room,
a charming little lamp-lit place, where one
could stage a play, or live an interesting life.

halloween: the hydrant dare

■ *George Roberts*

no eggs put behind the garage to rot
no shaving cream   no soap

something holds them back
says no   to getting things ready

and now   as a ghost of winter
invades their breath   and little folk
scurry through the falling dark
scrut and heimer and heimermann walk out
into the gaudy geometry of this night

wheels turn inside their bellies
they are loose   open

ready

they amble under a frosted moon
caught in low branches   until
the dull gleam of a pipe wrench
forgotten on a neighbor's step
gives them direction

the hydrants

winded   laughing
they sit in the tower grill
stomachs aching with the joy of it

imaginations racing
with the trail of streaming hydrants
they left behind

they do not speak
but gloat   and gulp air

devonna and michelle know something is up
and slide   like cats   into the booth

heimer and heimermann know they will walk these girls home
and fall all over eachother to spin the tale

> *first*
> *we stood/still as/statues*
> *taking it all/in*
>
> *later/we ran*
> *from the foaming/water*
> *lifting/into the/street*

the lights and sounds in scrut's head
go dead as a tilted pinball machine at the arcade

his ears burn
like candles in a pumpkin

moons leap in the girls' eyes
and the five go out
to find the wrench

but this time there is no magic
no spark leaping the dark space
    between them
and the shadow of a car   waiting
freezes them in its spotlight

> the running/the hedge leaping/the darkness
> brings back/for a moment/the quick breath
> of surviving

but when they meet in sumner park
there are only four

devonna squirming in the squad car
gives all the names   almost before
she catches her breath

in school the story grows
but scrut knows   as heimer and mann know
the glory is flat

the captain's words
> *one more time   boys*
> *and your asses will be racked up*
> *on meat hooks over at the plant*

still ringing in their ears

but ringing louder   their own
> *yes sir*

canceling what was left of the private
>   joy of those first dozen hits

and now   sitting in the back of algebra class
their separate thoughts of how it could have been
drain away like the last drops of water
as the hydrants were closed

How I Went Truant from School to Visit a River

■ *Mary Oliver*

There was a small river ran by our town.
It ran unguessed south by the setting sun:
Snake with green wings, it took all forest with it.
Birds sat and laughed upon the townward thickets;
Fox was a scarlet blink along its shores.

When school bells rang, I crept the echoing halls,
Slipped like a needle out of doors, and ran.
So sly! Like colt I leaped in a blond gambol.
But wonder warmed my cleverness to sleep,
And I went ferreting as any scholar

Where fish like nails with rainbows on their sides
Mulled in pools and herons dipped and poised;
Where feral berries glistened under thorns,

Where green leaves sighed the grammar of their hour
And bloodroot bloomed like alabaster verbs.

Noon stroked the sparrow's head with a windless thumb;
His mathematics drifted down the air.
The far bells tolled; I watched the wing's clapped drama;
I lolled beside the fine geometry
Of blue and wet-legged herons turned to stone.

Ah, still the dead bells sing, of some Pericles
Barefoot once along some marvelous river,
Of herons and the calm bird-havening trees,
In strophes like waterfalls, through the otherwise
Muttering ruins enclosing the dust of a child.

Anne Frank

■ *Sheryl L. Nelms*

I played hooky once

to see
if I could do it

it wasn't much fun
because the only
place I knew
to go

was home

then Dad showed up
in his squad car

and I spent
the afternoon
huddled in my closet
reading *The Diary of Anne Frank*

by flashlight

Confession to Mrs. Robert L. Snow

■ *Gary Soto*

I can clear my name.
It was my brother, not me,
Who stole your fruit
And sold that pop
Bottle on your porch,
Nickel for his pocket
And a jawbreaker that
Shattered like a star
When Mother got us home,
Naked with our two sins.
It was my brother, not me.
I was saintly that
Summer, inside and out,
And walked in puddles
In a Catholic sweater,
Even though it was
Summer and no school.
Good on Sundays,
I could jump from a chair
And spell my name three times
Before I dropped to my feet.
I jumped from the fence,
The incinerator, the house
—air all around for
Seconds and me flapping
As I spelled the holy
Countries of the world,
Yugoslavia as best I could.
My brother watched,
Sister with a jawbreaker
That was yet another
Bottle from your porch
Watched with fangs
Of candy in her mouth.
They witnessed me hang
In the air. They shouted

For me to fly over the tree,
Your tree, and come back
With yellow-green apricots.
I leaped beyond the clothes
Line and found myself
In the bush, knocked with
Lumps where a halo would rest?
I touched this sparkling hurt
And ran inside to ask Mother
What was hurting me.
Horns, she said
With her witch's mouth,
Devil horns! My sweater
Went limp on my body.
That did it. To hell
With the saints! I kicked
Puddles as I walked
To your house, not flew,
And let the apricots
And pop bottles alone.
While you watered
The front yard, I sneaked
Through the back door
And took a happy dollar
From your purse.
I laughed into my hands.
Horns, I whispered,
Big horns for me.

Mrs. Perkins

■ *David Allan Evans*

Mrs. Perkins wherever you are,
alive or dead:
I want you to know
I never laughed on your
son Jimmy's birthday
30 years ago.

In your basement that
smelled like moldy potatoes,
you put us on chairs in
a circle and turned out
the light to play "Dead Man."

"This is a dead man's *eye*,"
you said, and passed it
through our hands.
I knew it was a wet olive.
Cooley whispered it,
and laughed.

"This is a dead man's *ear*,"
you said, and I felt something
thin-rimmed.
A dried-up apricot.

Then a string bean for a finger
came around, and Cooley,
Bob and Jimmy broke up,
and ignorant Heeren laughed
so hard so long somebody
flicked the light on.

There you were, Mrs. Perkins,
clutching your face crying,
an open sack balanced on
your skinny, shaking knees.

Mrs. Perkins, I never laughed.

I would have taken anything
you handed to me,
and taken your word for it too.

The Telling Tree

■ *Linda Peavy*

"I'll race you to the telling tree,"
she called past clang of recess bell,
then sped to be the first of three
to claim the oak whose tangled roots,
sprawled angular as spiders' legs,
were shelter enough for secret things.
Shedding thin coats, they dropped onto
the hard-packed clay, legs out,
backs leaned against worn trunk,
coats snugged across them, blanket-like,
till yellow-brown plaid, dark navy, and red
were spread from root to rough, gnarled root
against the late November chill.
With only their faces out and free
there at the base of the telling tree
they shared the things they could not share
anywhere except that place.
Fran's mother was having a baby again.
Lee's dad had beaten her till she screamed.
Norma Jean's brother was back in jail.
And everyone knew that Freddie would fail
third grade and have to repeat next year.
And maybe you didn't go straight to hell
if your teeth touched the host—
but maybe you did,
and for other things, too. On and on
the secrets flew—nobody caring if anyone knew
all that they had to say to be free
there in the roots of the telling tree.

Apology

■ *Lynn Emanuel*

Tonight I lie staring into the unlit neighborhood
And remembering Maria Bauder at whose windows
I threw stones from behind a trellis of dead roses.
She was German and that year school resurrected
The war in Europe until all night long trains
Of dead children flashed past like light
On a hypnotist's gold watch. It has been a long time
Since that evening when, full of sulk and swagger,
I leaned in my mother's dormer watching as Maria entered
From her bare yard to ours filled with the soft
Exaltations of light. From the branches of black
Walnut the great weight of the moon leaned out.
I overheard her accusations and then came down
Into the issuance of my name and stood on the porch
In the chilly updraft of self-pity and said I was sorry
Under a sky tall and decorated with stars as a general.

A War Baby Looks Back

■ *Jonathan Holden*

In the tender years of Eisenhower's first
term, I started mine
in Dr. Swain's office, my jaws pried wide,
my gums stuffed with cotton cigarettes,
staring sadly up into a soft, fluorescent
light while Dr. Swain peered down in
and frowned. I had to wear elastic bands
that caught in my mouth on steel hooks;
to wash my abhorrent, plastic bite-plate
off each night until my teeth were
straight. It was all worth it.
Thanks to Dr. Swain, one spring evening
toward the end of Eisenhower's second
term, on the cold leather of my parents'
car, a girl named Tina
let me feel her up.

Liberty

■ *Ron Ikan*

Her name is on the tip
of your tongue,
the thought of her
soft as crushed velour.

Your first serious touch
took place second row from the back
of the Rialto balcony. . . .

She could have married you
but she didn't,
could have floated in on the tide
of your dreaming.

74

Close your eyes
in any theater rotunda
and inhale the salt-sweet brine of popcorn.
See, she's there still: Barbara Sue
Underwood. Ginny Heydecker.
Jane Niblock. Each one.

We loved you, girls.
We gave you everything.

Fishing

■ *Leo Dangel*

We have caught nothing, fishing all day
for bluegills in the Wolf Creek Dam,
when Arlo hooks and hauls in a carp,
big as a young hog. On the way home,
we decide to stop and show the fish
to the Peterson sisters—we'll use
any excuse to visit Charlene and Yvonne,
who are in the yard, carrying buckets
of skim milk to feed the pigs.
Yvonne always makes me feel a warm ache
all over, even now, especially now,
in her pink shorts smudged with dirt
and sweat-stained halter top.
I want to caress the bright red scratch
on one of her luscious thighs.
Arlo bends over the trunk of the Ford,
lifts out the carp, cradled in his hands,
and shoves its head toward the girls.
They squeal and jump back a step.
Arlo says that carp are friendly fish—
their lips are in the shape of a kiss.
Arlo says he will give Yvonne a quarter
if she'll kiss the carp. Yvonne says, "Yuck."
"Come on, Yvonne," he says, "kiss the carp.
Fifty cents, Yvonne, kiss the carp.

One dollar, Yvonne, come on, kiss the carp."
And then Yvonne leans forward, balanced
on her dainty tiptoes, her arms drawn back,
showing off her breasts, and those precious,
pouty lips touch the lips of the wet fish.
Yvonne tells Arlo to pay up. He tosses
the carp into the trunk and shows her
the empty pocket of his plastic billfold.
Yvonne says, "Oh you," and pounds Arlo's chest,
but not hard. He grabs her shoulders,
and they fall, laughing and wrestling
on the grass beside the yard light pole.
It's ridiculous when you think about it.
I would have paid Yvonne a dollar to kiss me.
I've got to hand it to Arlo though,
sometimes he really has a way with women.

Not Quite Kinsey

■ *Gary Hyland*

Magoo's the first to report
authentic backseat encounters
having dated Hot Pants Drake
off and on   *Mostly on, ha-ha*

His first car's a '49 Ford
and after only three days
a brassiere's slung from the aerial
a real roomy job, maybe 38C

He explains it's a trophy
of his first conquest in the car
and naturally we're impressed
Hey, Magoo, that musta broke your wrist

Who was she—Gina Lollamaidenform
You can get BUSTED for flashin that
But in a week it's no big deal
till one day we're parked at the A

Up comes Mrs. Magoo, his mother
short, fat, huffin like a steam engine
So that's where it went she hollers
She grabs a strap and yanks away

bending the aerial almost to the hood
I have this vision of his old lady
with a brassiere in her fist
zoomin over the city like Wonder Woman

But Magoo hops out and pulls it down
She jams it into her purse snarlin
Get straight home you little shit
and storms away down the street

Magoo sits red-faced for a while
his head against the steerin wheel
then pops up, grins and says
Anyone else wanna date with my old lady?

To Impress the Girl Next Door

■ *Ronald Koertge*

I go everywhere underground. It is a burden I have
imposed on myself: I want to deserve her love.

Accordingly when she goes out, I begin to dig; the
tap of her heels on the pavement drives me on.

Occasionally I come to the surface behind the gas
station and pass her on the street. "Hi there!"
She never nods, which is as it should be since

she does not know who I am or that—for her—
I live to burrow or how at night, curled in the
end of my present tunnel, I think about her

pretty feet and giggle in the rooty air and
go to sleep.

generations

■ *Sam Cornish*

he had a name
and no father
packed his books
in milk crates
never reading them—just watching
the colors in the afternoon dust

his clothes were patched jersey
he had nothing to say
but watched the strangers
across the street
listened to the fights upstairs

when he was thirteen
he found the yellow seasons of summer
were dark rooms
where girls undressed for boys
he found love in the smooth face of a girl
that has since become darker
and carried more children than he had freckles

he would come into her cold apartment
wondering if he had the special knowledge
that women wanted from men
endured the pain she moaned
the odor between her breasts

and wanted god to remember
he was young

and in much trouble

with himself

The Yes and the No, Redondo

■ *Greg Pape*

Look west and there's the sun
going down to sit
on the pan of the Pacific.
Look east and there's the haze
of freeways, the crown of industry,
the amber blanket of bad air
over the city that can't sleep
for dreams and the need
to dream. Straight up
the sky is still blue.
There's a small constellation
of daystars flashing, jets
in formation for a routine
pass over the Channel Islands
where the seabirds whiten
the rocks and the seals grovel.
To the pilots all this
is beautiful and abstract.
They can't smell it.
Look down, as a child would,
into the water where perch
are nudging barnacles on the pilings.
They swim in and out of sight
at ease in their silent bodies.
Perch are hard to hook, but kids
catch them and fishermen use them
for cut-bait. The gulls clean up.
The gulls glide around us
like the hours, or rock on the water,
small arks of attention
among fishing lines and floating debris.
The *City of Redondo*
with its load of fishermen
is rumbling out toward
the big mouth of South Bay.
But it's not the fishermen
I want you to see. It's that
boy standing on the roof
of the bait shack above

the sign that says "No diving
from the pier." He looks
at the man standing below him.
Talk me down if you can,
he thinks, go ahead, try.
Then he looks out over the Pacific.
The waves wash up the beach,
steel brushes on a snare
tuned tight. He'll fly
through the air, he'll see his baby
tonight, rock 'n' roll
in the surf of her
till he's out of breath. That's her
over there at the railing, calling,
fly boy, do a trick,
I'll keep you warm, take you home
give you something good
that you don't got.
You can't hear that
because she's talking with her eyes.
So go ahead, he thinks, call the cops.
Pull me down. Go ahead, try.
Today's the day he finds out
about his own yes and his own no.
Desire and distance fill him
as he leaps into the air,
frightening the gulls.
She loves the way he keeps
his arms spread his chest out
as he falls, against the law, forty feet
into the green waters of South Bay.
The way he enters the water
like a slick knife
with hardly a splash.
And she tells him so
as she greets him now
in the shadows among the pilings
under the municipal pier.
And later she will do her best
to keep all the promises
that shine in her eyes.

Camp Calvary

■ *Ronald Wallace*

The pastor's son, and only kid I know
at this damn camp, is off
necking with a counselor who's eighteen.
He's twelve. What does she see in him,
I wonder, as I trudge alone to archery
or crafts, to make a bull's-eye for
my mother, who sent me here
for God knows what perverted reason.
It's church camp. Every morning I pray
to be delivered from the squealing kids
who seem to be having such great fun
as I lie in wait inside my puny body
for time to pass and let me out.
What quirk of fate, what evil-minded
God has stuck me here? And does he sit
chuckling in his heaven, as water balloons
whiz by my ear and my name takes shape
and sails out over the lunchroom
like a straw paper dipped in mashed potatoes
sticking to the ceiling for everyone to see?
He's a pockmarked, pimply kid, skinny
as a cigarette, smelling of smoke and mint.
He carries booze in a hip flask
and sells dirty pictures of his sister.
And what does it matter that his father
will one day be unfrocked, his mother
become the loony I always knew she was,
Vietnam, cocaine, and the Navy take him away
for keeps? Today he's gone off with the counselor,
and everybody loves him, and I am
climbing out of my midget's body, cursing,
and heading for the future
just as fast as the mind can see.

Setting the Traps

■ *David Jauss*

Sun just up, mist rising
   off the Minnesota.
A month into spring and snow
still caught in shade so thick
   it holds the wind.

I'm fourteen and I pray
mink bleed in my traps.

■

Pale in the white bed,
my friend Steve stares
at the Daisy BB gun,
   my foolish present,
as if it is something
strangely embarrassing.

Leukemia, chemotherapy, laetrile.
Everything my parents say
sounds odd. *We know how
you'll miss Steve.*

   Miss. Steve.

■

   In dreams
a muskrat swims deep,
the trap's chain trailing
its bleeding paw and I
follow him down, eyes closed
   and mouth open.

   But at school
I tell my friends I'm a trapper
and show off my new
   buckskin jacket.

■

The track team runs past
the hospital in red sweats, breath
    exploding in the air.
I can't bear to see
that building. The earth
    disappears
stride by stride beneath my feet.

■

The frayed sleeve
of his woolen overcoat.
    His wet gloves
steaming on the radiator.
The Beatles record he played
    until it was static.

■

All the traps are beaded
    with dew.
I kneel to bury them
with loose grass and dirt,
make sure the chain is staked
    deep in the ground.

My hands tremble some.
    I don't want
anything to get away, a leg
missing, mouth bloody
with sacrifice.
    I refuse
to let anything get away.

    I am fourteen
and I will never die.

Anthony

■ *Jane Shore*

Your absent name at roll call was more present
than you ever were, forever
on parole in the back of the class.
The first morning you were gone,
we practiced penmanship to keep our minds
off you. My fist
uncoiled chains of connecting circles,
oscilloscopic hills;
my carved-up desk, rippled as a washboard.

A train cut you in half in the Jersey marshes.
You played there after school.
I thought of you and felt afraid.
One awkward *a* multiplied into a fence
running across the page.
I copied out two rows of *b*'s.
The caboose of the last *d* ran smack against
the margin. Nobody even liked you!
My *e*'s and *f*'s traveled over the snowy landscape
on parallel tracks—the blue guidelines
that kept our letters even.

The magician sawed his wife in half.
He passed his hand through the gulf of air
where her waist should be.
Divided into two boxes, she turned and smiled
and all her ten toes flexed.
I skipped a line.
I dotted the disconnected body of each *i*.
At the bottom of the page,
I wrote your name. Erased it.
Wrote it, and erased again.

The Pioneers

■ *Charlotte Mortimer*

The Pioneers had
The best of this country
The boy said.
They grabbed all the
Adventure, Indian-fighting,
      danger.
Since, it's been Dullsville.
And he rushed out to his car
And tore down the road
Doing sixty, maybe
And came around a curve
Behind an old Pontiac
Carrying two Barona Indians
Slow-moving, twenty thereabouts.
Overloaded from a scavenging
Trip to the dump.
And the fine pipe for fences
They were taking to the
      reservation
Pierced the boy's skull,
Removing a scalp-lock, neatly
And they buried them both, the
      boy
Inside the stockaded Mem'ry
      Garden
And over the fence, in
Joe Both's car dump
His faithful Mustang.

Elegy for the Girl Who Died in the Dump at Ford's Gulch

■ *Joan Johnson*

1

They forbade this place alone to us. My parents,
Ever reasoning, ticked off the dangers: snakes,
Tangled in the kudzu; rusted nails, refrigerators
Like coffins; ivy blisters; tramps; potholes;
Broken glass. A girl had died there once, slow
Smothering when a clay bank collapsed on her. Although
I did not know her, I practiced holding my breath
For weeks, glad at last of my lungs' helpless force.

2

Hide-and-seek held such dangers. Pop-the-whip thrilled
With its cruel gush of breath from the centrifugal
Whump of the end body. Scissors, paper, and stone
Left me bruised for days with punches from bad guesses.
I had retched from dizzy whirling on a dare. In truth
We were watchful of the jagged, the creeping, the hidden
Places when we plundered that gulch like a foreign country.

3

In the shell of a Hudson I found a Victrola
And twenty-seven records. My sister danced
Like crazy with me, giggles stitching our
Guts when the voice wound down. We swigged
An inch of gin judiciously, chewing wild mint
To kill the smell. We shrieked at a snake
Skin, the gulch bottom sand fooling our silly eyes
With glitter so that we thought we saw it
Slithering. We cast off a broken doll, the skull
Of a cat's carcass, and a string of green glass
Beads to make the dry skin whisper with a stick.

4

Dared, I could not refuse to fondle it, like paper,
Like strands in Mother's wig, like the taste
In my mouth when I held my breath too long. My parents
Would have warned me that where there is a skin
There is a snake. Dead girl, your lesson was
Against hiding in shaded caves. Those games taught me
To turn over warm rocks with a long stick, the shape
Of poison ivy leaves, the racket like flies that swarms
In my head when I've spun too long. And, yes, you taught
Me to be glad of seeing gold spots from looking
At the sun, glad of wary parents and quick lessoning.

The Teenage Cocaine Dealer Considers His Death on the Street Outside a Key West Funeral for a Much-Loved Civic Leader

■ *Jim Hall*

The biggest funeral this town
ever saw. You wait, this is
small potatoes. Bahama drill team,
Junkanoo bands, Cadillacs from here
to Miami, gridlocked in grief.
Every flower in Florida picked.
The sparkle gone from lovers' eyes.
The mayor and governor speechless.
Shore leave canceled, bars closed,
cost of living adjustments revoked.
My mother rocking in her chair, so
surprised at all the hullabaloo.
Just like Kennedy, they won't ever
forget the afternoon they hear it.
Everything'll close for a year.

All my friends, my many associates,
sniffing and sniffing the rest
of their measly lives.
They'll call off the evening news.
Ground all the jets. I'm serious.
You ask anybody they know Dino.
This isn't nothing, you wait.

Boy, Fifteen, Killed by Hummingbird

■ *Linda Linssen*

Bent low over the handlebars,
Arms arced and legs pumping
As his father had taught him
When he was five,
The boy struggled to pedal
Up Camelback Hill,
But he didn't mind
Because he knew that,
Once there, he could relax
And coast the rest of the way home.

He didn't see it hanging there
Dead ahead in the air,
Its tiny wings whirring invisibly,
Until it was too late.
The hummingbird poised itself
So that when the boy,
Speeding downhill,
Met the bird,
Its greedy bill
Exploded his right eye
Like a ripe cherry tomato
Skewered at a barbecue
And sent the liquid
Streaming down his cheek.

People said the father
Refused to accept the coroner's report
That the bird,
Seeking nectar,
Had pierced the boy's brain,
Abloom with youth,
And lodged there,
Draining it dry.
But a week later,
A neighbor watched the father
In his backyard
Hover over his hollyhocks
And, wielding a long knife,
Sever their heads.

Playmate

■ *Keith Wilson*

And because
of him, the small box carried at shoulder
height, high school boys somber in
black and cracking no smiles missed
football practice, stood, the heavy
little box rubbing one shoulder, awkward,
bearing down

From the church—singing.
I pulled the collar of my pea jacket tight,
I sat across the street in the cold winds
preceding spring trying to imagine Charlie:
him letting anyone keep him in that satin box.
All that crying, and him hating roses, getting
dressed up when it wasn't even Sunday, lying
there, in that sissy box.

That Summer

■ *Herbert Scott*

That summer nothing would do
but we sink the boat
in the heart of the lake
and swim in the cool night
for the yellow fire on the beach.

Through the dark water.

We all made it but Ronald,
whom we never found,
who was never Ronald
again; each fish I catch
since, I ask, Ron, is that you?

The House on Buder Street

■ *Gary Gildner*

My father found it after the war—
five rooms and two long rows of purple grapes
beside the picket fence in back
—which Eddie Hill, holding his jewels, leaped
the night we peppered a township
cruiser with bird-shot cut
from shotgun shells and stuffed in our BB rifles.

Every summer my mother made grape jelly
and Eddie, who had it down pat, polished my curveball.
Up in his attic we gagged on rum-soaked Crooks;
he described taking a flashlight to bed
and crawling under the sheets
the nights he slept with his older half sister.
Our houses were back-to-back.

The Buder Street brain was Jerry Skellinger.
He had a wing like a chicken
but could figure a Tiger's average without a stick or paper.
Once throwing darts I got him in the shoulder.
His father taught math and after school put peacocks
and roses in blocks of clear plastic.
They had a black cocker named Silly.

The night my brother was born
my father and I slept in the basement—
on Grandma's brass bed hauled down from the farm.
I was afraid of spiders
and clung to his back.
My aunt Sophie came from Detroit and steamed bottles
and made my sister and me eat everything.

I thought I'd be a doctor.
I took a kitchen knife and cut the cry
thing from my sister's doll. She screamed.
My aunt sighed, Be constructive.
I filled a can with pollywogs from Miller's Pond.
I watched Shirley Fox bite her warts.
Shirley came from Arkansas; her parents hated Catholics.

When my brother could toddle he climbed
a ladder and fell on his liver.
Then he picked up hepatitis.
When he got on his feet we lit sparklers
and buried hot stones to bake potatoes.
Shirley's warts were gone, too.
She'd lifted a robin's egg and rubbed on bloody bird.

Now we needed a bigger house.
Bigger also meant better.
My mother hated the dusty unpaved street,
the soot from the coal-burning furnace;
and her fruit cellar was packed!—
she couldn't can another pickle.
Some nights my father slept in our room.

The fall my mother insisted I still needed
long underwear, I threw them at her.
My father knocked me down,
then grabbed a long-handled hammer
and began to hit the house.
The rest of us cleaned up the chips.
By winter we had a new bedroom.

In the spring Shirley's breasts appeared.
Eddie worked on my slider and Miller's Pond
was filled in to build what my father called cracker boxes;
they were painted orange and lime and raspberry sherbet.
Some of Shirley's kin from Arkansas moved in one.
They went to work for Fisher Body, like her father,
and called each other shop rats.

My sister and I attended the Catholic school—
everyone else went to public. Eddie reported
that Shirley crossed her legs in Algebra; he figured
to make All-County and carried Trojans in his wallet.
My mother counted the Baptists on the street.
My father called it harping.
Sunday drives meant looking for a lot.

Indian Trail

■ *Bruce Guernsey*

The career of our play brought us through the dark muddy lanes
behind the houses where we ran the gauntlets of the rough
tribes.—JAMES JOYCE

This is not a poem about Indians.
I know nothing about them,
being from the suburbs of Boston
where the last Indians were probably burned
with the witches at Salem.
We lived on a narrow street
in my grandparents' old brown house;
it had bright shutters
and a large front porch
where, during a scrap, my best friend Henry
once clouted me on the head
with my own cowboy pistol.

In the smoke of late afternoons my grandfather
would lead Henry and me
down our street of gray lawns,
past the voices on the screened porches
whispering like priests, guiding us safely
by Mrs. Burner's pet mutt growling like Cerberus,
to the park's tennis courts
and the small patch of woods beside them.

Here, where the new high school
was later to be built,
he'd show us the path
where Indians danced all night
in our minds, their painted faces
flashing like jack-o'-lanterns by the fire.
Into this first world
we ran with drawn guns,
or, when Henry couldn't come,
as my grandfather waited,
I'd walk the dark trail terrified,
a pilgrim wanting to make peace.

I seldom saw Henry after he hit me
and later
after my father came back from the war,
we moved away.
The old house was eventually sold
and my grandfather,
always at ease with the darkness,
we laid to rest in Florida,
where, they say,
there are still real Indians
deep in the winding Everglades.

Jim

■ *Jonathan Holden*

When Uncle Jim came back from World War II
there was something wrong with him.
He hid behind sunglasses, and he sulked.
He was sultry as an afternoon with thunderheads.
We hardly saw him. He stayed in the sour
little room upstairs my parents kept for him.
An entire summer Jim moped there, shades
drawn, sprawled in the yellowing rubble
of his sheets, studying the ceiling
and working on his schemes while the hot

little radio beside him gagged with static
and Mel Allen's play-by-play of Yankee games.
The only time he peered out, it was to pad
downstairs to the kitchen for a beer.

My father's simian-faced and spare,
a scientist, he is severe.
His mouth is as definite as a trapdoor.
He never knew how to do anything but work.
He still knows the third conjugation of Latin
verbs by heart. It scared him almost over
into hatred to have his younger brother
lying up there day after day not doing anything.
He didn't show it. He stumped about his business,
bought the beer. At night he'd read.
He rarely talked to me.

Jim knew the things I had, at nine,
to know: the nestle of an M1's butt,
how hard it kicked, the ground speed
of the Lockheed F-80 Shooting Star,
how in artillery you had to yawn
so your ears wouldn't be hurt
when a howitzer went off. He taught me
how to talk cocky to take care of a bully,
DiMaggio's average, and all the junk
that Eddie Lopat threw.

Each week my father drove Jim to Madison,
where Jim leapt up on the two-car
Lackawanna train that carried him
sadly into Irvington to see his bookie,
Hoppie, and a VA psychiatrist.
Jim had this dream that he'd disappear
for years, swore when he drove back he'd tow
an extra golden Cadillac for Father.

His last summer with us, I remember Jim
outdoors, swimming vaguely like a drowning man
around in molten light, still implacable
behind his shades as he and Father

sweltered together, swinging at bedrock
for the swimming pool, swatting mosquitoes
between blows. Each evening Jim prodded
me and my new J. C. Higgins bike down
the driveway to where the road glimmered
like a brook, stagnant under the thick
banks of the bushes. In the green,
backed-up water of the twilight,
Jim taught me how to swim.

Gripping the bike seat's nape
at the bottom of my back, Jim held me up.
Together we treaded water toward Pardees' trees.
Jim jogged along beside me, then let go.
I'd flounder, fighting the sticky fists
of that tin Ferris wheel until the thing
outwrestled me and pinned me down;
but just as I was about to drown on gravel
Jim's hand was there to stand the evening
up again and steady it.

Once, Jim let go. With one thrust I
surged. Somewhere ahead of me a great
dam burst, the whole backed-up current
of the evening began flowing with delicious
little lapping sounds around me.
My bike was sweeping me away downstream.
I was alone and swimming in slow, steady
strokes, not sure quite where I was,
but Jim's hand wasn't there.
I couldn't even hear his feet,
I didn't care.

I could push the bushes past,
I could make the road roll under me in swells,
pump that road up into choppy waves
that seethed beneath my tires, beat
gently against the bottom of my seat.
I could make the woods beyond the bushes march,

the whole world gradually move in synchrony
before I let the bike spill out from under me,
crash like an armful of dishes.

When Jim moved to Irvington that fall
to make his fortune, he left his radio beside
the bed. My parents papered his old room
for me with bucking cowboys.
I sent him a letter with my drawing
of an M1. I never got one back.
We never heard from Jim again.
It didn't matter to me much, not even then:
I'd learned from him all I had to know.

Bus Depot Reunion

■ *David Allan Evans*

just over the edge
of my *Life* a young sailor
bounds from a Greyhound's
hiss into his mother's hug,
steps back, trades hands
with his father, then turns
to an old, hunched man
maybe his grandfather—

no hand, no word goes out,
they regard each other,

waiting for something, and
now their hands cup,

they begin to crouch
and spar, the old man

coming on like a pro,
snuffling, weaving,

circling, flicks
out a hook like a lizard's tongue,

the boy ducking, countering,
moving with his moves,

biffing at the bobbing
yellow grin, the clever

head, never landing a real
punch, never taking one

until suddenly, exactly
together they quit,

throw an arm around each other
and walk away laughing

Killing Chickens

■ *Bruce Weigl*

Never mind what you think,
The old man did not rush
Recklessly into the coop the last minute.
The chickens hardly stirred
For the easy way he sang to them.
Red sun is just burning out
Past slag heaps by the mill. The old man
Touches the blade of his killing knife
With his fat thumb.
I'm in the backyard on a quilt
Spread out under the heavy, dark plums
He cooks for his whiskey.
He walks among the hens singing
His chicken song way down in his throat
Until he finds the one who's ready
And he holds her to his barrel chest.

What did you think?
Did you think you just jerk the bird
From her roost and hack her head off?

Beyond the coop
I see the fleeting white dress of my grandmother
As she crosses and recrosses the porch
To fill the bucket with scalding water.
How easy the feathers will come
When she drowns them for plucking
And clouds the air with a stench
I can't stand not to breathe.

I'm not even a boy yet but I watch
The old man sing out into the yard,
His knife already at the chicken's throat
And everything begins to spin in my world—
He slices off the head without a squawk
And swirls the bird in circles, a fine
Blood spray fanning out far enough
To reach me where I wait
Obediently, where I can't stop watching.
The head the old man picks up,
His free hand become the puppet chicken
Clucking at me, pecking my head with the cold beak
Until I cry for him to stop
Until he pins me down, clucking, laughing, blood
All over his hands.

He did it so I would remember him
I tell myself all these years later.
He did it because it was his last summer
Among us. In August he didn't feel the fly
Come into his cancerous ear and lay its eggs.
He didn't feel the maggots hatch
As he sat dazed with pills in the sun.
He pecked my head and laughed out of love,
Out of love he snatched me roughly to his chest
And sang the foreign songs
Way down in his throat.

Explaining

■ *David B. Axelrod*

My grandmother's living room was dark
when I sat with her, except for the glow
of the Emerson TV, round 12″ screen.
We were pressed together in her old
velvet chair, the coarse blue pile itchy
where my pajamas parted between my
shirt and bottoms. The glass doors
were shut to stop the drafts. Over our

laps she pulled an old black fur, worn
so thin I could feel the backing, grown
brittle though lined with silk. The show
was probably "Amos and Andy" or "Manasha"
or "Mrs. Goldberg," and Nanny somehow
never quite understood. I was eight
or nine. I would explain to her
in detail until she said she knew. But
as I think of her, her hard-skinned hand
squeezing my arm, her sometimes sour
breath, her very soft loose skin on her arms,
I remember she never laughed no matter
how the joke was told or retold, and in the dark
I sat ashamed and lonely.

Cleaning the Well

■ *Fred Chappell*

Two worlds there are. One you think
You know; the Other is the Well.
In hard December down I went.
"Now clean it out good." Lord, I sank
Like an anchor. My granddad leant
Above. His face blazed bright as steel.

Two worlds, I tell you. Swallowed by stones
Adrip with sweat, I spun on the ache
Of the rope; the pulley shrieked like bones
Scraped merciless on violins.
Plunging an eye. Plunging a lake
Of corkscrew vertigo and silence.

I halfway knew the rope would break.

Two suns I entered. At exact noon
The white sun narrowly hung above;
Below, like an acid floating moon,
The sun of water shone.
And what beneath that? A monster trove

Of binding treasure I imagined:
Rib cage of drowned warlock gleaming,
Rust-chewed chain mail, or a plangent
Sunken bell tolling to the heart
Of earth. (They'd surely chosen an art-
less child to sound this soundless dreaming

O.) Dropping like a meteor,
I cried aloud—"Whoo! It's *God
Damn* cold!"—dancing the skin of the star.
"You watch your mouth, young man," he said.
I jerked and cursed in a silver fire
Of cold. My left leg thrummed like a wire.

Then, numb. Well water rose to my waist
And I became a figure of glass,
A naked explorer of outer space.
Felt I'd fricasseed my ass.
Felt I could stalk through earth and stone,
Nerveless creature without a bone.

Water-sun shattered, jelly-
bright wavelets lapped the walls.
Whatever was here to find, I stood
In the lonesome icy belly
Of the darkest vowel, lacking breath and balls,
Brain gummed mud.

"Say, Fred, how's it going down there?"
His words like gunshots roared; re-roared.
I answered, "Well—" (*Well well well . . .*)
And gave it up. It goes like Hell,
I thought. Precise accord
Of pain, disgust, and fear.

"Clean it out good." He drifted pan
And dipper down. I knelt and dredged
The well floor. Ice-razors edged
My eyes, the blackness flamed like fever,
Tin became nerve in my hand
Bodiless. *I shall arise never.*

What did I find under this black sun?
Twelve plastic pearls, Monopoly
Money, a greenish rotten cat,
Rubber knife, toy gun,
Clock guts, wish book, door key,
An indescribable female hat.

Was it worth the trip, was it true Descent?
Plumbing my childhood, to fall
Through the hole in the world and become . . .
What? *He told me to go. I went.*
(Recalling something beyond recall.
Cold cock on the nether roof of Home.)

Slouch sun swayed like a drunk
As up he hauled me, up, up,
Most willing fish that was ever caught.
I quivered galvanic in the taut
Loop, wobbled on the solid lip
Of earth, scarcely believing my luck.

His ordinary world too rich
For me, too sudden. Frozen blue,
Dead to armpit, I could not keep
My feet. I shut my eyes to fetch
Back holy dark. Now I knew
All my life uneasy sleep.

Jonah, Joseph, Lazarus,
Were you delivered so? Ript untimely
From black wellspring of death, unseemly
Haste of flesh dragged forth?
Artemis of waters, succor us,
Oversurfeit with our earth.

My vision of light trembled like steam.
I could not think. My senses drowned
In Arctic Ocean, the Pleiades
Streaked in my head like silver fleas.
I could not say what I had found.
I cannot say my dream.

When life began re-tickling my skin
My bones shuddered me. Sun now stood
At one o'clock. Yellow. Thin.
I had not found death good.
"Down there I kept thinking I was dead."

"Aw, you're all right," he said.

Code Blue

■ *Billie Lou Cantwell*

three times they called
and I knew
why they needed doctors in ICU
Grandma knew it too
but didn't look up
from the handkerchief she twisted in her lap
I held tight to my mother's hand
and wondered if the pounding in
my chest would ever stop

it wasn't what I expected
this hurry-up and commotion
I thought death would be reverent
dignified and special
like Grandpa

First Job

■ *Jim Daniels*

My mother paid me a nickel
for each cricket I caught.
Looking down the stairs,
nursing my baby sister,
she wanted them silent, dead.
My brother sulked, wanting
to trap, release.

I hunted by sound, stalking them
among old newspapers, broken toys,
trapping them under a cup.
I showed each one to my mother
who sat on the sagging couch upstairs
burping the baby.

Dangling in air, they spit
on my hands as I dropped them
in the toilet, watched them dance
on the surface, swirl away.

I sat in the cool, damp basement
and listened to the silence
of a job well done.
I rubbed the coins together
and made a sweet sound.
I rubbed and rubbed
but no one came.

Bowling Alley

■ *Michael Van Walleghen*

There were six lanes
and a bar next door.

We worked two lanes
at a time. "Jumping"

it was called. Two
maybe three leagues

a night @ 13¢ a line
plus tips. It added up.

It was even kind of fun—
like being on a ship

and dodging broadsides
from the enemy. *Look*

lively lads! Right on.
You had to pay attention.

Otherwise a freak ricochet
could knock your teeth out.

And it was hot back there
concussive, sweat-slippery

a place I'd dream about
for years—an atmosphere

whistling with bombs
as I remember it

grapeshot, cannonballs
all the furious shrapnel

transposed and manifest
of beleaguered adolescence. . . .

No wonder we got tired.
There was so much smoke

by the end of the night
we could hardly breathe—

we needed air back there
stars in the open hatchway

an icy, offshore gale
crashing on the gun deck . . .

until BANG we were done
the last pin racked

and we found ourselves
taking a leak in fact

out beside the Dumpster
in the literal alley

where it sometimes snowed.
One of us, I remember,

had a tattoo. One of us
was missing some teeth.

One for One

■ *Jim Heynen*

There was this old woman down the road
who grew snakes in her garden
and paid us to kill them.
We'd do it
with sticks that had forked nails in the ends.
We'd slam these down on snake heads
and bring them squirming alive to her
in plastic sacks.
She stood in her doorway,
a little puffy when she saw them,
writhing rainbows of garters
blaming each other for their misery.
We killed them for her with the sticks
and draped them on clotheslines
where she'd count them.
Ten cents apiece.
She always had Sunday collection dimes
saved in a cookie jar.
She shared these with us
and we made good with them
down at the local candy store.

Old Shevchenko

■ *Peter Oresick*

I recall him, plainly, in his black wool suit
and his yellow shirt buttoned at the collar.

After evening bells, he'd stroll
until dark, and at corners
he'd quote from the Gospel; a mumble
on the breeze, an angel in black,
drawing laughs from passersby.

I saw him once encircled by *Los Barbados*,
seven bearded men on motorcycles. He glared
at their skull-and-bone insignias.
Pocketing his bifocals, he unbuttoned his shirt
and doffed his black fedora. From his neck
he lifted a block of painted wood—
the image of the Black Madonna.
                                    It dangled
from a bootlace, then he shook it at them
and passed from their midst unharmed.

This was in the 60s, when I was a boy,
and given to searching for signs. I looked
to the sky, to crumbling gray clouds,
where the blue appeared like a beautiful eye.

I sat and looked around me
and listened. The leaves overhead
scarcely rustled; by their delicate noise
I have trusted my life.

Black Dog, Red Dog

■ *Stephen Dobyns*

The boy waits on the top step, his hand on the door
to the screen porch. A green bike lies in the grass,
saddlebags stuffed with folded newspapers. The street
is lined with maples in full green of summer, white houses
set back from the road. The man who the boy has come
to collect from shuffles onto the porch. As is his custom,
he wears a gray dress with flowers. Long gray hair
covers his shoulders, catches in a week's growth of beard.
The boy opens the door and glancing down he sees yellow
streaks of urine running down the man's legs, snaking
into the gray socks and loafers. For a year, the boy
has delivered the man's papers, mowed and raked his lawn.
He's even been inside the house which stinks of excrement
and garbage, with forgotten bags of groceries on tables:
rotten fruit, moldy bread, packages of unopened hamburger.
He would wait in the hall as the man counted out pennies
from a paper bag, adding five extra out of kindness.
The boy thinks of when the man's mother was alive.
He would sneak up to the house when the music began
and watch the man and his mother dance cheek to cheek
around the kitchen, slowly, hesitantly, as if each
thought the other could break as simply as a china plate.
The mother had been dead a week before a neighbor found her
and even then her son wouldn't let her go. The boy sat on
the curb watching the man hurl his soft white body against
the immaculate state troopers who tried not to touch him
but only keep him from where men from the funeral home
carried out his mother wrapped in red blankets, smelling
like hamburger left for weeks on the umbrella stand.

Today as the boy waits on the top step watching the urine
trickle into the man's socks, he raises his head to see
the pale blue eyes fixed upon him with their wrinkles and
bags and zigzagging red lines. As he stares into them,
he begins to believe he is staring out of those eyes,
looking down at a thin blond boy on his front steps.

Then he lifts his head and still through the man's eyes
he sees the softness of late afternoon light on the street
where the man has spent his entire life, sees the green
of summer, white Victorian houses as through a white fog
so they shimmer and flicker before him. Looking past
the houses, past the first fields, he sees the reddening
sky of sunset, sees the land rushing west as if it wanted
to smash itself as easily as a cup is thrown to the floor,
violently pursuing the sky in great spirals of red wind.

Abruptly the boy steps back. When he looks again into
the man's eyes, they appear bottomless and sad; and he
wants to touch his arm, say he's sorry about his mother,
sorry he's crazy, sorry he lets urine run down his leg
and wears a dress. Instead, he gives him his paper
and leaves. As he raises his bike, he looks out toward
red sky and darkening earth, and they seem poised
like two animals that have always hated each other,
each fiercely wanting to tear out the other's throat:
black dog, red dog—now more despairing, more resolved.

Gregory's House

■ *David Huddle*

It was a testimony
to something that
could make my daddy
mad even talking about
it, how when one side
of the house collapsed
they just stopped using
those rooms, and when
the front porch dropped
off Gregory was upset
because he had to do
his drinking in the
kitchen with the kids
whining all around him

and the TV turned up so
loud he couldn't half
concentrate. And they
say when the outhouse
folded over one January
Gregory cut a hole in
the floor and was happy
not to have to make that
trip in cold weather.
But every Saturday
morning they sent out
one dirty-fisted child
to pay me for the paper.
Until that Sunday I
threw a heavy, rolled-up
one too high and up onto
the roof, and it fell
right on through, and
the next Saturday Gregory
himself came out to the
fence and cussed me and
said I owed him damages
for knocking a hole in
his house.

Zora

■ *Jessie Schell*

Rubbing the naked white of our legs
with her skinny black hands—
those bent licorice sticks
that flailed the waters
on our dripping heads—
Zora:
like a witch's pot,
like the infinite black under cellar stairs.
The terrible whites of her eyes
rattled the gourd of her head.

112

She would promise
to eat us whole if we misbehaved,
to lick our white bones clean
in the light of tomorrow's moon.
She would soap our skin
with the scourge of her cloth,
and croon the ritual to its end:
singing to us of Jesus,
of all her friends,
who were washed in the blood of the lamb.

Old Mag

■ *Joyce Hollingsworth-Barkley*

The first black woman
        I ever knew
came in the back door
of Granma's kitchen.

I touched her hand
and looked at my finger.

Born the year of
        the Surrender
was the only birth date
she could remember
as she muttered over
turnip greens in the sink
or grumped her way
to the ironing board,
her sword tongue switching
inside her teeth.

Old Mag,
why are you so mean?
Why do you swat at me
when I reach for tea cakes
to stomachache on
in the chinaberry tree?

Why are your eyes
gnarled like that
when I'm sitting
on the doorstep
and it's time for you
to throw out dishwater?

Is it because I wondered
if you'd rub off on me
or because no other white child
ever touched you?

Black Patent Leather Shoes

■ *Karen L. Mitchell*

Slipping in my black patent leather shoes
Papa would make sure they reflected
Me
Not caring how many times they were
Used
He would make me put them on
With laced stockings
I never danced in those black leather
Shoes
Only studied their simple details:
Black
As black as my hair they surely were
With three straps, that held me there, and heels
Stacked
And I could not wear my black leather
Shoes
Every day, but only once or twice a
Week
And he would make sure black polish was
Used
Papa would make sure those shoes
Reflected me

The Age of Reason

■ *Michael Van Walleghen*

Once, my father got invited
by an almost perfect stranger

a four-hundred-pound alcoholic
who bought the drinks all day

to go really flying sometime
sightseeing in his Piper Cub

and my father said *perfect!*
Tomorrow was my birthday

I'd be seven years old, a chip
off the old daredevil himself

and we'd love to go flying.
We'd even bring a case of beer.

My father weighed two-fifty,
two-seventy-five in those days

the beer weighed something
the ice, the cooler. I weighed

practically nothing: forty-five,
maybe fifty pounds at the most—

just enough to make me nervous.
Where were the parachutes? Who

was this guy? Then suddenly
there we were, lumbering

down a bumpy, too short runway
and headed for a fence. . . .

Holy Shit! my father shouts
and that's it, all we need

by way of the miraculous
to lift us in a twinkling

over everything—fence, trees
and power line. What a birthday!

We were really flying now....
We were probably high enough

to have another beer in fact,
high enough to see Belle Isle

the Waterworks, Packard's
and the Chrysler plant.

We could even see our own
bug-sized house down there

our own backyard, smaller
than a chewed down thumbnail.

We wondered if my mother
was taking down the laundry

and if she'd wave.... Lightning
trembled in the thunderheads

above Belle Isle. Altitude:
2,500, air speed: one-twenty

but the fuel gauge I noticed
quivered right on empty....

I'd reached the age of reason.
Our pilot lit a big cigar.

My Father's Fortune

Silence was my father's fortune,
carried with him everywhere for safekeeping,
houses and cars and offices crowded with silence.
And trailing my father

four fair-skinned children of different sizes,
a matched set of luggage,
silence folded inside like Sunday clothes.
Everything my father owned transporting silence.

But not a silence of anger or isolation.
Instead, one of yearning, inarticulate
and fumbling. A silence that learned
its own language, its own stubborn love.

Tableau

■ *Keith Wilson*

I remember my father, holding his cocker spaniel,
both sinking deep into a pool of quicksand.
We were walking together when he, in his way,
went his way, leaving me to find them later.

He had heard Daisy yelping, found her caught
and leaped in to save her. For a moment I couldn't
believe he'd actually done it, my desert and river
wise father, but there they were, slowly going down
as the sun also sank.
                It took me an hour to get them out,
reaching out my hand from a rock on the shore, helping him,
still holding the dog, to edge closer to safety. By the time
he was clear and free, Daisy barking at the sands,
it was almost dark and we picked our ways out of the Bosque
beating with sticks against the ground to let the rattlers

know we were coming. Whack! And the buzz would come close
by, then slightly farther away. Whack! and more would
rattle, the cool evening bringing them out to hunt.

He sent Daisy ahead of us finally, because she could smell
better, he said, though the cucumber musk of snake seemed
everywhere to my nostrils, as we climbed up the final bank
and headed for the old car parked against the growing
darkness, my father walking out like John Wayne after
a gun battle, Daisy and I trailing along behind.

On This, A Holy Night

■ *Kevin Bezner*

You ruined the Christmas tree.
You pulled off the tinsel wrapped
from branch to branch. You threw
glass ornaments at the wreath
above the fireplace. Reds, blues, greens,
yellows popped like burning wood.
I couldn't say a word

as pine needles, tinsel, the colored glass fell
to the floor harder than the snow outside.
I ran out the door. I stood cold and coatless.
I watched through a window and listened
as Mother's loud complaints made you drunker.
You said you could take no more,
there was no other woman,

you would drink whatever you wanted,
you weren't drunk—this was drunk.
You broke everything, everything
but the tree itself, which stood,
a skeleton with cracked limbs,
its remaining strands of tinsel
brushed by streetlight.

My Father's Leaving

■ *Ira Sadoff*

When I came back, he was gone.
My mother was in the bathroom
crying, my sister in her crib
restless but asleep. The sun
was shining in the bay window,
the grass had just been cut.
No one mentioned the other woman,
nights he spent in that stranger's house.

I sat at my desk and wrote him a note.
When my mother saw his name on the sheet
of paper, she asked me to leave the house.
When she spoke, her voice was like a whisper
to someone else, her hand a weight
on my arm I could not feel.

In the evening, though, I opened the door
and saw a thousand houses just like ours.
I thought I was the one who was leaving,
and behind me I heard my mother's voice
asking me to stay. But I was thirteen
and wishing I were a man I listened
to no one, and no words from a woman
I loved were strong enough to make me stop.

■ *Kate Daniels*

My dolls came alive in it,
all of them whining in unison.
And there was a pink curtain.
I'd part it and see your hand
flailing the bedroom window
beckoning me in.

But my dolls needed me, too,
wetting their little diapers,
mewing Ma-Ma whenever I thumped
their stomachs.
I pretended my hair was long
like yours, draped a black towel
over my head and nuzzled the dollies
till it fell over them
covering their faces.

Each of us in our houses:
I thought of you combing your hair
before the mirror
chatting about men who had loved you,
how my father was a fool,
what you wished you had done.

I never knew why you wanted me.
I was alone out there. I loved you
away from the specter of your black hair
gleaming in the mirror, your lovely face
talking to itself.

Mamaw and Frank

■ *William Burt*

Proud woman
My Mamaw
She stood out
Among the poor people
Of Clarksdale
Like a diamond
Among stones
Severe
Straight-backed
She prepared to go
To the post office
As a soldier
Prepared for battle
Black cotton dress
Buttoned at the throat
Her long witch's hair
Carefully pinned up
Before the dresser mirror
She pulled herself tall
Turning this way
That way
Glaring
Daring the mirror to say
One blessed thing
Proud woman
My Mamaw
Stern
No time for foolishness
Rigamarole
She called it
Mamaw never in her life
Said I love you
But she wrote it on every moment
We spent together
In her living room
Dark and cold
Playing cards

Telling ghost stories
Giggling with excitement
Precious thing this
Silly childish love
Between a little boy
And an old woman
This stern old woman
In her black cotton armor
With her old cardboard Bible
And her steadfast distrust
Of all grown men
Mamaw's husband Frank
Was homely
And cross-eyed
But soft inside
Like the sweet potatoes he grew
All the neighbors
Would say
Mr. Swayze
Oh I hate to ask
But this back of mine
So if you would
Could you possibly
See your way clear
To carry me here
Carry me there
Do this
Do that
Do the other
Oh thank you
Mr. Swayze
What would we ever do
Mr. Swayze
Rigamarole
Mamaw would snort
They're just making a big
Fool out of you
Frank Swayze
And he would duck his head
Pained at displeasing her
I loved Frank

Who smelled of tobacco
Which he hand-rolled
Or else spat
Into a peach can
Frank never had two dollars
At the same time
His whole life
But he jingled with pride
At the Chinaman store
And bought me bright red sodas
I thought Frank was rich
Mamaw snorted
And leaned back in her rocker
And opened her Bible to Revelations
She read about Satan
Coming to earth every thousand years
Last time it was Hitler
She told me soberly
Now it's Martin Luther King
I said nothing
I knew she was wrong
And it was the worst kind of knowing
Like a place inside me
That couldn't get warm
I was twelve
Past easy reach of childhood
Mamaw looked at me
Over her Revelations
With a look she reserved for the neighbors
And grown men
I'm not really older
I wanted to say
I'm just bigger that's all
Frank came home
From the Chinaman store
Drunk as a boar
He vomited on the linoleum
Mamaw rose indignantly
You're killing yourself
She scolded
One more can of beer

And you'll be dead
Frank Swayze
Dead
A drunkard
She followed him
Into the kitchen
Don't put that beer
In my box Frank Swayze
Look at you
How much did you spend
On that slop
He bent beneath her words
Like a hatless man
In a rainstorm
Falling back
Against the sink
Seeing the can there
He tore it open
Reared it like a weapon
I
Flew
Through
The
Air
Grabbed it no I cried no
What are you doing
He said dully
I'm taking it you'll die if you
Drink it you'll die
What do you care he
Said not letting go I
Care because I love you
I cried and the can
As cold as anything
I'd ever touched
Came away
From his hand
I poured it
Down the sink
Mamaw helped me pour
Them all down the sink

And later
I lay awake
In the dark
On the couch
In the living room
Remembering
Card games
And ghost stories
Giggles of excitement
And sodas of bright red
Forever gone
Forever cold
Like the place inside me
Aching dully
I knew it would never
Get warm again
Not really

Secrets

■ *Linda Schandelmeier*

She slits empty feed sacks
shows me
how to fold the cloth strips
pin them
to my panties to catch
the blood.
She has been watching me
waiting
for the bleeding I kept
secret
for over a year, not
wanting
to tell, not wanting to be
like her.

Summer Mama

■ *Anne Keiter*

I can remember coming home
on soft summer afternoons,
the loose screen door gently banging
behind me,
shutting out the world
of skinned knees and warm clover;
welcomed summer days
of endless hummings of
June bugs and bike wheels.
Coming in to the
sunny-as-outdoors indoors,
I'd listen for just a second
to the change of sounds:
replacing the June bug's song
was my mother's,
soft and light,
bouncing against the yellow
kitchen walls and clean muslin curtains.
Then the warmest smile
that ever came fresh
from a too-old oven,
and the warmest eyes
that ever learned favor
in a southern garden,
would sneak a glance
around the carefully painted door.
And taking in at once
my burnt nose and
summer tarred feet,
those arms that could open so wide
and gather in the whole room
if they wanted,
would fold around
just me.

The Runaway Girl

■ *Gregory Corso*

Ever since running away from home
somebody real weird tailed her:
it's been her constant paranoia.
Like a bug, it hugs close to the ground.
And no matter where she walks, it follows her.

In the distance behind her
she can hear her mother calling, calling;
yet she cannot turn around.

Runaway Teen

■ *William Stafford*

Any cold night I am hiding. Some people
come along. They stop on the bridge
and I listen. Water gurgles
and sings, but voices are clear as moonlight.

"We'll keep it for all of us—
the others don't need to share."
"How about Connie?—she wanted to be here."
"Forget about her." And they walk on.

In freezing rain that night I choose
my place:—in the wilderness, the loyalty
of chance. In time's clumsy attempts
anything can happen, and faith is a relic today.

It's hard being a person.
We all know that.

Acknowledgments

While every effort has been made to secure permission, it has in a few cases proved impossible to trace the author or author's executor. Permission to reprint poems is gratefully acknowledged to the following:

ATHENEUM PUBLISHERS, an imprint of Macmillan Publishing Company, for "Smoke" from *For the New Year* by Eric Pankey, copyright © 1984 by Eric Pankey.

DAVID B. AXELROD, for "Explaining" from *White Lies* by David B. Axelrod (La Jolla Poets Press), copyright © 1988.

BOB HENRY BABER, for "Fat Girl with Baton."

BEACON PRESS, for "Generations" from *Generations* by Sam Cornish, copyright © 1968, 1969, 1970, 1971 by Sam Cornish.

KEVIN BEZNER, for "On This, A Holy Night," first published in *Passages North*.

BKMK PRESS, for "Mrs. Perkins" and "The Antelope" from *Real and False Alarms* by David Allan Evans, copyright University of Missouri, Kansas City, MO.

BLACK SPARROW PRESS, for "Poetry Lesson Number One" from *Heavy Daughter Blues: Poems and Stories 1968–1986* by Wanda Coleman, copyright © 1987 by Wanda Coleman.

GWENDOLYN BROOKS, for "Gang Girls" from *Blacks* (The David Company, Chicago), copyright © 1987.

WILLIAM BURT, for "Hank and Peg" and "Mamaw and Frank."

TERESA CADER, for "The Strand Theatre."

BILLIE LOU CANTWELL, for "Code Blue" (Porch Swing Rhyme).

HENRY CARLILE, for "Dodo" from *Running Lights*, copyright © 1981 by Henry Carlile, reprinted by permission of the author and Dragon Gate, Inc.

CARNEGIE-MELLON UNIVERSITY PRESS, for "Black Dog, Red Dog" from *American Poetry Review* by Stephen Dobyns; and "Preposterous" and "The Teenage Cocaine Dealer Considers His Death on the Street Outside a Key West Funeral for a Much-Loved Civic Leader" from *False Statements* by Jim Hall, copyright © 1986 by Jim Hall.

JO CARSON, for "Jump."

CHRONICLE BOOKS, for "Confession to Mrs. Robert L. Snow" from *Who Will Know Us* by Gary Soto, copyright © 1990.

CITY LIGHTS, for "The Runaway Girl" from *Gasoline and the Vestal Lady* by Gregory Corso, copyright © 1955, 1958 by Gregory Corso.

MOLLY MALONE COOK LITERARY AGENCY, for "How I Went Truant from School to Visit a River" from *No Voyage* by Mary Oliver.

COPPER CANYON PRESS, for "One for One" from *A Suitable Church* by Jim Heynen, copyright © 1981 by Copper Canyon Press.

H. R. COURSEN, for "Sister" from *Rewinding the Reel: New and Selected Poems* (Cider Mill Press, Stratford, CT, 1989).

LEO DANGEL, for "Gaining Yardage" and "No Question" from *Old Man Brunner Country* (Spoon River Poetry Press), copyright © 1987 by Leo Dangel; and "Fishing" and "The Love Nest."

KATE DANIELS, for "The Playhouse" (originally appeared in *Plainsong*, Western Kentucky University Press, Bowling Green, KY).

J. M. DENT & SONS, LTD., for "How I Went Truant from School to Visit a River" from *No Voyage* by Mary Oliver.

DAVID ALLAN EVANS, for "Ronnie Schwinck" from *Poetry Now*.

SALLY FISHER, for "News for the Cafeteria."

GRAYWOLF PRESS, for "The Mad Nun" from *Daily Horoscope* by Dana Gioia, copyright © 1986 by Dana Gioia.

BRUCE GUERNSEY, for "Indian Trail" from *January Thaw* (University of Pittsburgh Press, 1982).

GEOF HEWITT, for "Eagle Rock" from *Just Worlds* (Ithaca House Books), copyright © 1989 by Geof Hewitt.

JOYCE HOLLINGSWORTH-BARKLEY, for "Old Mag" from *Honeysuckle Child* (Poet's Palate).

HOUGHTON MIFFLIN COMPANY, for "My Father's Leaving" from *Palm Reading in Winter* by Ira Sadoff, copyright © 1978 by Ira Sadoff; and for "Young" from *All My Pretty Ones* by Anne Sexton, copyright © 1962 by Anne Sexton.

GARY HYLAND, for "Zip on 'Good Advice,'" "How It Was," "Not Quite Kinsey," and "Their Names," from *Just Off Main* (Thistledown Press, Saskatoon, Canada), copyright © 1982.

RON IKAN, for "Liberty."

DAVID JAUSS, for "Setting the Traps" (originally appeared in *The Florida Review*).

JOAN JOHNSON, for "Elegy for the Girl Who Died in the Dump at Ford's Gulch" from *Poem*, with the permission of Huntsville Literary Association.

ANNE KEITER, for "Summer Mama."

WILLIAM KLOEFKORN, for "During the Sermon ..." from *ludi jr*, (Platte Valley Press, 1983).

DORIANNE LAUX, for "Rites of Passage," copyright © 1990 by Dorianne Laux.

LINDA LINSSEN, for "Boy, Fifteen, Killed by Hummingbird" from *Minnesota Ink*, Spring 1987.

WILLIAM STAFFORD, for "Runaway Teen."

RODNEY TORRESON, for "Howie Kell Suspends All Lust to Contemplate the Universe" (originally appeared in the *Mankato Poetry Review*).

ERIC TRETHEWEY, for "Rescue" from *Dreaming of Rivers* (Cleveland State University Poetry Center), copyright © 1984 by Eric Trethewey.

UNIVERSITY OF ARKANSAS PRESS, for "To Impress the Girl Next Door" by Ron Koertge, copyright © 1982.

UNIVERSITY OF GEORGIA PRESS, for "Apology" from *Hotel Fiesta* by Lynn Emanuel, copyright © 1984 by Lynn Emanuel.

UNIVERSITY OF ILLINOIS PRESS, for "Bowling Alley" and "The Age of Reason" from *Blue Tango* by Michael Van Walleghen, copyright © 1989 by Michael Van Walleghen.

UNIVERSITY OF MASSACHUSETTS PRESS, Amherst, MA, for "Jim" from *The Names of the Rapids* by Jonathan Holden, copyright © 1985 by Jonathan Holden; for "The Winter They Bombed Pearl Harbor," from *After the Noise of Saigon*, copyright © 1988 by Walter McDonald; and for "Anthony" by Jane Shore from *The Minute Hand*, copyright © 1987 by Jane Shore.

UNIVERSITY OF MISSOURI PRESS, for "A War Baby Looks Back" from *Design for a House* by Jonathan Holden, copyright © 1972 by Jonathan Holden.

UNIVERSITY OF PITTSBURGH PRESS, for "The House on Buder Street" from *Blue Like the Heavens: New & Selected Poems* by Gary Gildner, copyright © 1984 by Gary Gildner; for "Gregory's House" from *Paper Boy* by David Huddle, copyright © 1979 by David Huddle; for "The Yes and the No, Redondo" from *Black Branches* by Greg Pape, copyright © 1984 by Greg Pape; for "Walking with Jackie, Sitting with a Dog" from *Where Sparrows Work Hard* by Gary Soto, copyright © 1981 by Gary Soto; and for "Zimmer in Grade School" from *Family Reunion*, copyright © 1983 by Paul Zimmer.

UNIVERSITY OF WISCONSIN PRESS, Madison WI, for "First Job," "For People Who Can't Open Their Hoods," and "Wheels" from *Places/Everyone* by Jim Daniels, copyright © 1985 by the Board of Regents of the University of Wisconsin System; and for "Music Lessons" from *Level Green* by Judith Volmer, copyright © 1990 by the Board of Regents of the University of Wisconsin System.

UNIVERSITY PRESS OF NEW ENGLAND, for "Stay With Me" from *Yellow Light* by Garrett Kaoru Hongo, copyright © 1982 by Garrett Kaoru Hongo; for "Sister" from *Masks of the Dreamer* by Mike Lowery, copyright © 1979 by Mike Lowery; for "Shaking" from *Sigodlin* by Robert Morgan, copyright © 1990 by Robert Morgan; and for "Trouble" from *Collected Poems* by James Wright, copyright © 1971 by James Wright.
